How does our society make it p
men will be violent to the wor

Jan Horsfall believes that both violence and masculinities are socially constructed.

She locates the phenomenon in a broader social context beyond individual biology or psychology, drawing out the links betweeen violence, gender constructions and power relations. She focuses resolutely on men and many of the connections she makes are new, or have previously been intellectually marginalised.

Horsfall investigates patriarchal structures and practices: the law, the social security–tax system, the employment-unemployment-wage system, and male ideologies which are embedded in professional practices.

The presence of the past also examines spousal power relations, the way emotional distance between fathers and sons creates low self-esteem and insecurities, and the way in which men with high emotional dependency needs abrogate parental responsibilities.

While such men deny responsibility for their behaviour, women are powerless to stop their violence. *The presence of the past* challenges men to begin taking responsibility for their actions and inactions, individually and collectively.

Jan Horsfall is Senior Lecturer in Community Health at the University College of Northern Victoria and lives in Bendigo.

Jan Horsfall

The presence
of the past

Male violence in the family

ALLEN & UNWIN

First published 1991
Allen & Unwin Pty Ltd
8 Napier Street, North Sydney, NSW 2059 Australia

National Library of Australia
Cataloguing-in-Publication entry:

Horsfall, Jan.
    The presence of the past: male violence
    in the family.

    Bibliography.
    Includes index.
    ISBN 0 04 442326 8.

    1. Family violence. 2. Women—Crimes against.
    3. Abusive men. I. Title.

362.8292

Set in 10.5/11.5 Sabon by Graphicraft Typesetters, Hong Kong
Printed by Chong Moh Offset Printing Pte Ltd, Singapore

Creative writing program assisted by the Australia Council,
the Australian Government's arts funding and advisory body.

Contents

Freud, the son, could no more remember the terror of father-violence than could Freud, the father, admit to such deeds.

Phyllis Chesler, *About Men*, p. 20

Dear Professor Freud,
...You go around...reducing everyone to the level of sons...who blushingly admit the existence of their faults. Meanwhile you remain on top as the father, sitting pretty...
Most sincerely yours, Jung.

Phyllis Chesler, *About Men*, p. 270

Preface

As a naive but alert counsellor employed in a community health centre in a provincial town, I became increasingly aware of the violence that some women had experienced. Husbands, brothers and fathers were emotionally, physically and sexually violent towards wives, sisters and daughters. Some profoundly violated women were pursuing their own tortuous paths towards becoming whole. But what were the men doing?

Ignorance for me was a powerful motivator. Books had helped me understand many issues over my lifetime. Working very closely with people on and off over a 25-year period provided me with a privileged exposure to people's private lives and some insights into our human condition. Over the next few years I read a lot of information of varying quality on male violence within the family. There are grisly descriptions of such violence, terrifying stories, accounts that are painful to read.

Approximately 60 per cent of the books, chapters and articles I read were written by women and the bulk of this material concentrates on female victims. Women writing about traumatised women is no doubt related to politicising the plight of the victims and processing the accumulated pain. This focus on women as victims is understandable but naturally fails to provide any coherent insight into men as perpetrators of violence.

Introduction

How does it happen that some men are violent towards the
women they love? How does it happen that some men rape
women they love and others rape women they have never spoken
to? How does it happen that some men sexually violate young
children whom they are raising, who may share their genes?
These are terrible questions. To attempt to answer them one must
uncover forbidden practices and face issues of cruelty, death, sex
and intimacy. It entails looking for the invisible, questioning what
is given and noting what is missing.

Many writings on male violence towards females throw some
light on the problem; however, others claim to be dealing with
male violence in a learned manner but end up as treatises riddled
with misogyny, weak excuses and doubtful logic. The genre of
written material which is most offensive is that which blames the
victim. Jean Renvoize's famous book *Web of Violence* is one such
book. Renvoize draws initially on early male researchers' work.
Snell, Rosenwald and Robey studied 'the wifebeater's wife', and
found her to be 'aggressive, even masculine'. A forensic psychiat-
rist (Faulk) studied 23 men who were awaiting trial for murdering
or attempting to murder their wives. Nine of these men described
their wives (who were not interviewed—after all, one-third were
dead) as argumentative and dominating. Scott similarly studied
40 such prisoners; in response to the fact that half of these men
were long-term wife batterers, Renvoize asks of these disenfran-
chised women (again some of whom were dead) why they did not
flee.[1]

Against such a background, Renvoize launches some of her
own victim-blaming hypotheses. The drunken man demands food
and then sex from his wife and she refuses one or both. Battered
women are not impartial and therefore they blame the men for
the violence! She perceives women as teasers and withholders of
sex.[2]

Unfortunately things get worse when we proceed to the incest
chapter. Girls in the latency period are often very sexually attractive, 'sometimes deliberately so'. Dr Arnon Bentovim explains
father–adolescent daughter incest by blaming the girl who feels 'a
need to regress to babyhood' and share her father's bed which
results in a relationship which becomes 'over-intense'.[3]

1

Natalie Shainess is a psychoanalyst who has written about battered women, rape victims and masochism. Unfortunately her latest book also highlights the contributions that she alleges the female victim makes towards her own 'demise'. She actually criticises Richard Gelles' extensive works on family violence in America because he omits 'one crucial factor...from his construct: the *victim's* personality and identity'. Victims are described as innocent, polite, friendly and obliging: presumably these are provocative qualities.

Again things deteriorate when Shainess shifts to the conjectural mode. She discusses a well-known American multiple murderer of women who was on death row when she wrote *Sweet Suffering*. Two male journalists asked the convicted murderer (who denied his guilt) to speculate about the sort of person who would commit such crimes. In this taped interview he states that he was disturbed and remorseful after the murders and decided to rape instead of murder. He found a young woman alone, wielded a knife and ordered her to submit to him. She argued with him and he killed then raped her. Shainess declares that the victim had 'signed her own death warrant'. Shainess discusses the rape and murder of a female violinist in an elevator at the Metropolitan Opera House by a male stagehand. She actually hypothesises that the victim verbally deflated the stagehand's frail ego and implies that she may still be alive if she had changed the subject to the more neutral terrain of music![4]

Jeanne Deschner, although not as well known as Renvoize and Shainess, manages to implicate the victim in her book *The Hitting Habit*, even after declaring early on that most victims do nothing to warrant such suffering. She states that women victims score more verbal points than their husbands. Some victims precipitate a violent incident because their male partners are 'nicer afterwards'. She believes some women are 'addicted to the soap opera-like excitement of the battering cycle'. Babies are not exempted, as their crying can 'unwittingly' initiate a spiral of violence by 'refusing to be quickly comforted'.[5]

Along with victim-blaming goes the provision of excuses for the male perpetrator. Again Renvoize comes to the fore. Sympathising with busy doctors, she explains away the extreme violence of half of Scott's murderers because of severe stress, guessing that they were on tranquillisers. She also considers pregnancy to be provocative and that women's concern for the foetus or child 'inflames jealousy' in violent men.[6] Regarding incest perpetrators, alcohol is a significant 'aid' in breaking the incest taboo— presumably only for incest perpetrators. Such men are 'highly sexed'—this is deduced from the fact that many are having sexual intercourse with their daughters, their wife and sometimes a mistress too.[7] According to Deschner and others, 'primitive rage' wells up in violent men, though this disregards the information from battered women that the blows are often so well directed that any evidence is covered by garments or hair.

Amongst Deschner's individual types of batterers are the 'social chaos' kind who are poor and come from generations of violence. Many batterers do come from such backgrounds, so do many victims; other batterers and victims do not. Another 'type', according to Deschner, are those whose response to crying and yelling is 'abnormal'.[8]

Mothers are often invoked as the cause of this male violence. According to Shainess, mothers may unintentionally damage their children and produce a victimiser. Such mothers may be manipulative, coercive and seductive, or inattentive, distracted and distant. This scenario gets worse. 'Men who strangle their victims most likely had mothers who were extremely controlling and who tried to shove things [food, concepts, points of view] down their throat.'[9]

This propensity for blaming the mother of a violent man for his wife battering, rapes and mass murders seems very indirect and illogical at the commonsense level. Unfortunately there is a lengthy intellectual tradition going back to Freud which encourages a mother focus. The most 'pathological' mothers were well promoted in the 1950s and 1960s: these were the schizophrenogenic mothers who created, apparently all on their own, schizophrenic offspring, especially sons.

The mother of the sexually assaulted child (wife of the perpetrator husband) is incorporated into explanations of incest by Renvoize and other writers. Renvoize quotes Professor Walters, the author of a book on child abuse, as claiming that the 'primary cause [of incest] usually rests on the relationship between the adult male and the adult female.' Renvoize goes on to portray the mothers of children who are sexually assaulted within the family as women who know about the incest and collude in some way with the men perpetrators. This is a particularly insidious version of mother-blaming in that the mother is implicated whether she knows about the incest or not, because if she says she does not know she might be lying, or the more sophisticated may claim she knows 'subconsciously'. The rationale for such a comprehensive damnation of wives of incest perpetrators is that the women prefer to keep the 'infidelity' in the family and, of course, some women 'dislike' sex. This is capped off by Walters' unwarranted claim that when the incest is exposed, the mother 'almost always' decides to keep her husband and send her daughter away.[10]

Mother-blaming authors excuse the perpetrators and blame the mother of the perpetrator and/or the mother of the victim. Such 'explanatory' models force me to note that the perpetrator is missing, and is excused in his absence. The main problem with these sorts of generalised claims is that often teachers who are not specialists in these areas are the ones that briefly cover areas of family violence in nursing, psychology, social work and welfare courses. Thus whole generations of practitioners have been given information about these emotionally demanding areas that is drawn from 'experts' like Renvoize and Shainess. Unless the students have time to explore the sources and 'research' on which writers have drawn, the information is accepted at face value. How relevant to family violence is data drawn from murderers on death row? How relevant is material from the 1960s and 1970s which was published as 'definitive' data before more sophisticated analyses of the inequalities of family power were available? How can practitioners 'help' violent families in an appropriate and fair manner when the credibility of the woman is undermined at the outset and the perpetrators are carefully camouflaged?

Interactionist literature leaves the victim-blaming, mother-blaming and perpetrator-excusing terrain and shifts to a rather more pleasant sounding 'responsibility-sharing' position. This too has its inbuilt biases and practical dangers. Renvoize's metaphor of the web of violence evokes ideas of entrapment, hopelessness and lack of responsibility.

> I have come to see violence more and more in terms of a gigantic web in which countless generations of people are caught. A violent adolescent who has just kicked in someone's teeth is yet one more creature snared in a web.[11]

Such a description has commonsense appeal. However, on closer scrutiny, such broad generalisations are unfair and unhelpful. Surely the proportion of females with low self-esteem is at least as high as that of males with low self-esteem. Are the women indulging in an equivalent amount of battering, rape and incest? The intergenerational explanation of overt violence is true enough but decreases the sense of hope for victims, perpetrators and 'welfare' workers. Some children of violent parents do not violate their own children; and some children of apparently nonviolent families do. Gender and power differences within the family are omitted from these interactionist approaches.

Deschner's subtitle for her book is *Anger Control for Battering*

Couples. This heading implies that two people are (and always were?) angry, both of them are out of control, or at least their anger is, and that they batter each other. Battering is usually a term that describes ongoing, severe physical assaults. In none of the family violence literature is there evidence that women are battering their men partners at anything like the same rate as the men are battering their women partners.

> Consort battering fits very well into the model of coercive exchanges building up to aggression by one party and forced submission by the other partner. The exchanges of nags and threats during the build-up phase clearly take the form of a coercion spiral. It hardly matters whether the husband or the wife initiated the first unpleasant event, for they both respond by trying to control the other person via escalation of negative remarks and threats, until one of them loses control and resorts to physical force to make the other one submit.[12]

This description conveys the view of two equally powerful, equally culpable, equally equipped people who tussle for supremacy under conditions in which either might be violent and 'win', or either might 'lose'. Victims of battering commonly say that the violence comes 'out of the blue' or that it was apparently in response to dinner being too hot or too cold. Thus there is no necessary exchange of threats. The threats and the violence are often one-sided. The forced submission of the woman victim is the most predictable outcome of these interactions. When this interactionist model is applied to adult rape victims and child victims, the pseudo-equality built into the 'explanation' becomes more blatant. Apart from the power of husbands over wives, fathers over children and cruising rapists over unsuspecting victims-to-be, we must remember that the average male is taller, heavier and stronger than the average female, let alone a child or adolescent.

A final explanation of male violence which has not been fashionable over the last decade, but which gains a guernsey on occasions still, is that male perpetrators of violence are 'pathological', different, almost psychiatrically disturbed. At least three of Deschner's individual types fit this label.[13] The mental illness type is the most obvious, and certainly a very small percentage of batterers, rapists and incest perpetrators are psychotic. Deschner claims that up to about 70 per cent of male batterers are 'pathologically jealous' as are fathers of adolescent incest victims. They certainly are jealous and perhaps their jealousy is so extreme that the word pathological promptly springs to mind. Unfortunately such a label conjures up notions of being genetically determined and beyond the control of the inhabited person.

Then we have Deschner's 'mental disturbance type'—a euphemism for 'personality disorder' which is a contentious psychiatric category. Generally people who are provided with this label are not psychotic or delusional, nor are they sad or anxious, but they have a very unsettling effect on the lives of people they are friendly with or live with.[14] I have no doubt that some proportion of batterers, rapists and incest perpetrators are sociopaths; but then we must question why a very high proportion of sociopaths are male. The term overlaps with many 'criminal' activities and in a way may be conceived as being defined by virtue of 'unacceptable' social behaviour. This circular way of deeming violence as abnormal, therefore violent people must be abnormal, is a pseudo-medical way of excusing the perpetrator and clouding his gender in jargon which makes it unclear what we are up against and whether the perpetrator is in a fit state to take responsibility for his actions.

These are the types of partial explanations of male violence that I uncovered over a number of years as I was grappling with an attempt to explain to myself how some men in our society are so devastatingly violent towards women they claim to 'love', or to children they are 'protecting'. It became clear that commonly held social beliefs permeated these models: commonplace but unexamined beliefs about women as naggers, female children as seductresses and female sexual partners as having no sexual rights; and such no-win beliefs as women who say 'no' mean 'yes'. The fact that such beliefs—and practices which emanate from them—exist leads me to remind myself that ours is a patriarchal society and misogyny is part of our man-made world.

What is wrong with much of the 'male violence' literature written by both men and women? It is one-sided. I have located only two books, Edward Gondolf's *Men Who Batter* and Daniel Sonkin, Del Martin and Lenore Walker's *The Male Batterer*, which focus entirely on male batterers. They both declare a practical approach in their subtitles,[15] with no in-depth interviews, personal scrutiny or other forms of dismembering or victimising. Where are the treatises exhorting men to be responsible, to stop being violent, to take charge of their personal lives? Where are the medical, psychiatric, psychological and sociological analyses of fathers? Where are the books written by men acknowledging their power over women in the public domain, their marital advantages, their sexual advantages, their violence? Where are the tracts in which they are introspective and soul-searching?[16]

What I have discerned in much of the literature on male violence towards females is:

- women in focus as the victim;
- women blamed for their own violation;
- mothers cited as the cause of male violence;
- interactions between spouses or family members instigating male violence.

What is patently missing is:

- the male perpetrator;
- males as responsible people;
- fathers, and fathers of sons;
- the patriarchal power of males over females, as understood by men.

In this book I address all four missing issues. Given that the perpetrator is missing, I assume I must look first under the cloak of patriarchy.

Men are historians, researchers, writers. How has it happened that these men have failed to study men who are violent to women? It cannot be an accident. Do these men deny such violence exists? Are they embarrassed? Are they supportive of it? Are they overwhelmed? Are they afraid of violent men? Whatever the answers, the net result is an effective denial of the violence and an abrogation of male responsibility for it. These two characteristics are exactly the characteristics of violent men!

This is patriarchal power at work. Men determine what is a social problem, what it will be called, how it will be studied and how it will be explained. At one level, women have named male violence as a social problem. This forces a crack in the collective denial. The practices have been described and named, but it is not enough. Men determine how it will be studied. Men (in the United States) carry out 'representative' national surveys, they develop 'conflict tactics scales', they grade violence from minor to severe.[17] Women join them.[18] Then some researchers explain it all by drawing diagrams with a large number of boxes (factors) with arrows going in every conceivable direction. All of the contributory factors have been noted, nothing is missed. But when one ponders this schematic representation of male violence towards females, one cannot discern what came first, which is more important. It has been 'explained' in a most compact, sophisticated and scientific manner.[19] The problem has been named, studied and 'explained' but in a superficial, bloodless, distant and perpetratorless way.

There is another way of conceptualising male violence towards females, and that is to have 'other' men take responsibility. Via this means, the most bizarre, criminal, deviant, sick and blatant (meaning those that are caught) men who have been violent towards women are dissociated from mankind and treated as male subjects for study. Murderers, convicted rapists, men who have left a trail of women victims are the marginalised men who are investigated. There is another variation upon this theme of men who have nothing in common with the untainted researcher and this is sociological distancing by researching street youths, violent subcultures and men from the working classes. Here group processes are implicated but the violent men are 'other' by virtue of age, ethnicity, culture, education, employment, class, poverty or family history.

The patriarchal underpinnings of the law, of medicine and of social sciences allow researchers, male and female, to divest the violent male of his responsibility. It is a truly amazing intellectual feat to think that a murderer may not be responsible for murder; that a batterer may not be responsible for severely injuring his wife; that a rapist may not be responsible for his sexual violence against a woman who was going about her daily business. This is where victim-blaming, mother-blaming and partner-blaming comes from. The illogical blaming is the overresponsibility which goes hand in hand with irresponsibility. Patriarchy gives men the power to take responsibility for what they choose to be responsible for and not for what they will not be responsible for. In our society, men deem it appropriate that they are responsible for the law, politics, profit and science. They abrogate responsibility for themselves, their children, the environment and their violence, amongst other things.

Continuing the theme that certain obvious aspects of male violence towards females have been omitted from the literature, I eventually realised that sex is missing. Gender is sometimes missing in 'spouse abuse', 'family violence' and 'marital violence', but most writers have recognised that it is the men who are being violent and the women who are traumatised. Sex in the sense of sexual practices is virtually ignored. We must remember that incest involves sexual practices, rape involves sexual practices and battering may include sexual practices. Battered women are violated by their sexual partners—that is, the relationship is sexual in an ongoing way, the violence may be sexual during battering or after other physical and emotional forms of violence. Incest, rape and battering are all violent. They are also all sexual.

In the literature on male violence against females, the male secrets I unearthed were low self-esteem and high emotional dependency. Low self-esteem was hard to discern at first, but many researchers are very much aware of it. High emotional dependency was hiding under a much thicker veil—this quality is evident to clinicians who work with violent men. Sex however was quite obfuscated. In line with the general focus on women, it was actually easier to find information about the sexual problems of battered women, rape victims and incest survivors than about the male perpetrators of these acts.

Having looked for answers, I found questions, absences and missing men. These are the themes which underly this work. I had assumed at the outset that Australian men are as violent towards women as their North American counterparts, and that this violence is condoned by our society. In 1988, the Office of the Status of Women surveyed a representative sample of 1504 Australian adults. This study revealed that 23 per cent of men and 17 per cent of women 'believe it may be justifiable for a man to shove, kick or hit his female partner if she does not obey him, wastes money, fails to keep the house clean, refuses to sleep with him or admits to sleeping with another man'.[20] It is disturbing to be informed that almost one-quarter of our fellow men accept a man shoving, kicking or hitting his 'partner'. Does she have reciprocal rights? Should her husband do what she says? Who has the power to determine what expenditures are a 'waste'. Presumably husbands have the power to determine how clean is 'clean' as well. Do some wives lose the right to sleep in another bed? Can a man refuse to sleep without his woman partner? Sex is probably the missing word again. Are wives demanding and getting sexual fidelity from their husbands? Patriarchy, under the mask of equality, is alive and well.

In the next chapter I discuss relationships between patriarchy and capitalism, and the public–private division in our society. Battering and incest usually take place in the privacy of the female's home as do some proportion of rapes. Institutionalised violence is background violence deemed 'normal', such as wars and some military and police practices. Some professions and the ramifications of their male-centredness are discussed. The patriarchal prejudices of the labour market, the tax system and welfare ideologies and practices are also highlighted. Male advantages deriving from these invisible structures support male violence.

I focus on the modern family in chapter 2.[21] I discuss stereotypical portrayals of women and men in our society and conclude that if such people did marry, they would have great difficulties relating to each other. These stereotypes are man-made, diminish our humanity and turn out to be impotent opposites. To prevent violence in relationships, common ground has to be established and similarities worked on. Then I look at some Australian studies of the division of labour at home where 'her' jobs and 'his' jobs perpetuate the gendered notions of difference and distance.

Chapter 3 is about male gender construction. This chapter is more original than the others. Here, within the modern family, I try to work out how boys are raised to become men and how this relates to the possible outcome of male violence. Having discovered that fathers have gone missing from child raising, I investigate what this means to sons. So this chapter is about fathers and sons.

Complex behaviours, like violating a female loved-one, cannot be explained by macro-social structures, ideologies and the family alone. They have to take the unconscious of the individual male into account. I discuss the unconscious and conscious ramifications for boys with 'distant' fathers. These fathers are emotionally distant from their children and that is experienced by the child as a rejection by the significant male in his life. This is a phenomenon which some Australian empirical studies (for example, Paul Amato's *Children in Australian Families*) have also observed.

In chapter 4 I discuss two major consequences for boys with emotionally distant fathers. One is low self-esteem because the boy does not feel that he is good enough for his father: the other is high emotional dependency because the boy has not received positive nurturance from significant males in his life. This emotional neediness becomes part of the male's inner life and is usually covered over because our man-made society demands that men should be 'independent'. Men who do not feel independent often pass as normal by presenting a 'macho' face to the world to hide their desperate need for affection. Such men (batterers) inappropriately expect compensatory 'love' to come from their adult female partners; others (incest perpetrators) demand intimacy from their children; and others (rapists) manifest these needs in violent sex.

Chapter 5 discusses what can be done to prevent male violence against females increasing. Such social change has to work at many levels. Thus I consider action in light of patriarchal social structures, the modern family, and male gender construction. These processes will take a long time, therefore refuges for women and children and other necessary supports must continue to be provided. Ultimately men collectively have to take responsibility for their violences; men will have to say 'no' to male violence against females as individuals; and men will have to assist each other to make these radical changes within and outside themselves.

1 | Patriarchal contributions to the construction of male violence

And, my gracious Duke,
Be it so she will not here before your Grace
Consent to marry with Demetrius,
I beg the ancient privilege of Athens,
As she is mine, I may dispose of her;
Which shall be either to this gentleman,
Or to her death, according to our law
Immediately provided in that case.

Egeus, father of Hermia, *A Midsummer-Night's Dream*,
William Shakespeare

PATRIARCHY AND POWER: DEFINITIONS

Ruth and Russell Dobash are the researchers who have made the connections between wife battering and patriarchy most explicit by publishing their major study in book form under the title *Violence Against Wives: A Case Against the Patriarchy*.

> [The] long patriarchal tradition...was explicitly established in the institutional practices of both the church and the state and supported by some of the most prominent political, legal, religious, philosophical, and literary figures in Western society...They believed that men had the right to dominate and control women and that women were by their nature subservient to men. This relationship was deemed natural, sacred and unproblematic and such beliefs resulted in long periods of disregard and/or denial of the husband's abuses of his economic, political, and physical power.[1]

They thus consider patriarchy to be an unexamined and complex system of beliefs and practices with a long history. These permeated institutional and individual beliefs and practices. Such pervasive domination of women by men has ramifications in political, legal, economic, religious and personal domains, including violence by a male against a female partner. 'The husband's

12

use of physical force against his wife was...an expression of the unequal status, authority and power of marital partners and was widely accepted as appropriate to the husband's superior position.'[2] The Dobashes believe that unequal power relations between the genders, in society at large and within marriage, lay the foundations on which the violence of husbands against wives may be built. Violence is one way in which men may 'express' their power in relation to women.

Even though the Dobashes and many other writers in the field of wife battering emphasise the contributions of patriarchy, they do not define these terms clearly. To begin my discussion of patriarchy, the following difficulties must be acknowledged. 'One of the major problems encountered in trying to understand the material and historical bases of patriarchy is that of conceptual ambiguity and absences in analysis.'[3] Also, there are four general aspects of the use of the term patriarchy which add to its lack of clarity. Firstly, the concept is often not defined but a whole explanatory argument is developed deriving from these less than explicit 'patriarchal' relations. Secondly, patriarchy is frequently presented as a universal set of relations. Thirdly, the term is a-historical or trans-historical; for example, some theorists claim that patriarchal relations preceded capitalism, but it is unclear whether they precede feudalism too. A final general problem with the use of the concept for analytical purposes is that often all social relations are reduced to patriarchal relations.[4]

Bob Connell appraises the realistic development of a 'theory of patriarchy' by stating that such theorising 'is far from being a tightly knit logical system. It is, rather, a *network* of insights and arguments about relations between various things...Its scope at any given time is defined by the reach of this network of arguments'.[5] Such a pragmatic approach itself can then be in danger of losing conceptual integrity, a problem Connell recognises himself. 'What entitles us to talk of a unity, a coherence, and system and hence "patriarchy", at all?'[6]

The literal definition of a patriarch, according to the Oxford English Dictionary, 'the father and ruler of a family or tribe'. Thus patriarchy can be deemed to mean 'rule of the father'. David Morgan argues that some aspects of this literal and 'older' understanding of patriarchy are pertinent to our 'newer' feminist analyses of patriarchal relationships. He considers that specific structural and relational similarities between father–child and husband–wife remain extant. Wife and child are 'dependents' and the husband–father has legal and financial obligations to support the dependent person in both relationships. In both instances the dependents work without pay for the benefit of the family as a whole and for the husband–father in particular. The relationships are also personalistic, and characterised by emotional ties. Thus, within patriarchal family relations, the father has access to legal, financial and emotional means of influencing and controlling dependent family members.[7] In both sets of patriarchal relationships, the father has considerable control of property and its disposal. Legal, financial and property rights of the father are the material facets of these patriarchal relationships.

According to Morgan, in a patriarchal society the husband has an emotional (affective) connection to his wife and *vice versa*, and he has greater access to a range of material resources. Given his institutionalised position of power vis-à-vis his wife, he may take advantage of her materially and emotionally. The battering husband whose wife does not work in the labour market for an income has the power to not provide her with enough money for food, rent or health care. He also has the power to emotionally blackmail his wife who is dependent on him affectively and materially, and he can manipulate her in relation to her role as he perceives it as nurturer of their children. Wife-battering literature emphasises that rates of battering are greater when the man is the sole income earner and when the couple have very young children. These two conditions are not necessarily the same: both denote the wife's material dependence, but the presence of young children may allow the husband to utilise his emotional power in relation to the children's emotional and material needs and vulnerabilities.

Thus we can see the material and emotional leverage a male batterer has in our society. The male non-batterer has the same power advantages in relation to his wife. Both the batterer and non-batterer live in the same political, economic and social environments. These gendered power relationships—that is, power differences deriving from one's status as female, male, child—within the family can benefit the batterer who takes overt advantage of this infrastructure; but the non-batterer can wield power in the same arenas without resorting to violence. Thus, patriarchal power differentials contribute to both the likelihood of male violence under these circumstances and significant advantages should the husband resort to violence.

Morgan's discussion of patriarchy does not make the gendered power relations sufficiently explicit. Gendered power relations are *the* essence of patriarchy and contribute to our understanding of men who are violent towards women. This then raises the question: How can power be defined? According to M Stacey and M Price

> ...power is clearly one element in all social relationships and is difficult to separate from such related concepts as authority, control, influence, and domination... The notion of power undoubtedly has to do with the ability of an individual or a group to influence the course of events in the direction they desire even against resistance by others.[8]

Peter Bachrach and Morton Baratz point out that any discussion of power cannot ignore the 'mobilization of bias... of the dominant values and the political myths, ritual and institutional practices which tend to favour the vested interests of one or more groups, relative to others'.[9] In our society, clearly the mobilisation of bias will be that of comparative male political, institutional and personal privilege deriving from patriarchy. The vested interests of powerful individuals and groups may never be challenged by virtue of institutionalised practices which prevent some problems from becoming 'issues'. This is what Bachrach and Baratz call the two faces of power: the visible and the less visible facets of power relations.

> A power relationship exists when (a) there is a conflict over values or course of action between A and B; (b) B complies with A's wishes; and (c) B does so because he is fearful that A will deprive him of a value or values which he regards more highly than those which would have been achieved by noncompliance.[10]

Bachrach and Baratz acknowledge that A's power in relation to B may be broad or narrow in 'scope'; it is invariably not absolute, that is the person with the power advantage is not always in control of the other.

Influence and power are similar in that they both have rational and relational attributes. 'But they are different in that *the exercise of power depends upon potential sanctions*, while the exercise of influence does not.'[11] The significant point here is that in a patriarchal society men have the power to utilise sanctions against women. Authority is defined as ' "a quality of communication" that possesses "the potentiality of reasoned elaboration" '.[12] B defers to A in this situation because B 'recognizes that the command is reasonable in terms of his own values'.[13] In a situation involving power, B defers not because of the logic of the demand but because deference is the safer way out.

Within the modern family, the husband frequently has the power to make decisions, even if they are against his wife's interests and she resists the implementation of the decisions. Of course husband–wife relationships in a patriarchal society work best for the husband and his superiority of power when he does not need to take active steps and she does not resist overtly. Then the power differential is part of the relationship and neither participant need ever be conscious of the processes which reveal the scope of his power in relation to her. To wield power over his wife, the husband must have some resources which she needs or wants and which he can withdraw, or threaten to withdraw, as a sanction. The sanction may be positive, in that he has the power to give her something she does want or put her in a position that she wants to be in if she accedes to his decision. The sanction may be negative, in that he has the power to manoeuvre her into a situation she does not want to be in unless she accepts his demands.

What resources might a husband have access to that he can withdraw as a sanction or dump on her as a sanction? If the woman is not in paid employment and they have children, he may withhold money, a car, clothes, food, himself, sex or any other resource that he considers she is dependent on. He may insult her, abuse the children, get drunk, bring disruptive friends home, batter her, demand more meals or sex or any other practice that he considers will demean her and encourage malleability. Amongst the repertoire of resources which he has greater access to is his own physical strength. On the average, men are taller, heavier, and stronger than women. Thus the strength to over-whelm a woman physically is a resource that almost all men have; and if they doubt this they still have greater access to weaponry and are encouraged to be more skilful with these resources, too. Violence is an ultimate resource available to all husbands who wish to wield overt power over their wives. The male batterer is a product of patriarchal relations and his practices are a sign that these relations are under duress either from outside and/or inside the family.

'[W]hen a system of power is thoroughly in command, it has scarcely need to speak itself aloud.'[14] Male batterers render patriarchy audible and denote that that system of power is not so thoroughly in command. The existence of wife battering makes the 'invisible' face of patriarchal power visible. If both men and women were well adapted to the patriarchal structures, men would have no need to exercise their superior physical power.

'The essence of patriarchy, then, can be seen as the ways in which power relations between men and women, and men and children, are exercised and defined.'[15] These power relations have

a long history and a momentum of their own. As John Westergaard and Henrietta Resler note

> ...in any society, the pattern of people's lives...take the forms which
> they do...in large part because certain social mechanisms...are taken
> for granted...The favoured group enjoys effective power, even when
> its members take no active steps to exercise power. They do not need
> to do so...simply because things work their way in any case.[16]

In our society the majority of men will therefore not have to
resort to naked forms of power-wielding because social practices
have evolved from patriarchal premises. Relations between husband and wife are unequal simply because they are, and always
have been!

Zillah Eisenstein is a feminist who successfully retrieves the
concept of patriarchy from some of its murkiness. Her definition
of patriarchy is that it is a sexual system of power in which the
male possesses superior power. She adopts the phrase capitalist-
patriarchy 'to emphasise the mutually reinforcing dialectical relationship between capitalist class structure and hierarchical sexual
structuring'.[17] She seeks to retain the distinctiveness of these two
complex spheres of social relationships and the adaptability of
both structures vis-à-vis each other.

The *thesis* of Eisenstein's argument is 'woman as class'. 'Power
or powerlessness derives from a person's class position; hence
oppression is a result of capitalist organisation and is based in a
lack of power and control.'[18] Oppression (class derived) and
exploitation (gender derived) must not be confused; but each
interacts powerfully with the other at many social and practical
levels.

Eisenstein's *antithesis* is 'woman as sex'. This is the 'radical
feminist' position that in our society our personality, our positions in the labour force and our relations with the state are
determined by our gender. 'The sexual division of labour and
society expresses the most basic hierarchical division in our society
between masculine and feminine roles. It is the basic mechanism
of control for patriarchal culture.'[19] The division and opposition
of genders is deemed to be more fundamental than class divisions in a capitalist society.

According to Eisenstein the *synthesis* of these two arguments is
achieved by the 'socialist feminist' approach to the location of
women in our society.

> Patriarchy (as male supremacy) provides the sexual hierarchical
> ordering of society for political control and as a political system

cannot be reduced to its economic structure; while capitalism as an economic class system driven by the pursuit of profit feeds off the patriarchal ordering. Together they form the political economy of the society.[20]

This synthesis integrates belief systems and economic practices. Thus Eisenstein explicates the relationships between class and gender and highlights their dialectical (interactional) relationships and adaptations over time.

MALE TOGETHERNESS AND FEMALE SEPARATION

Patriarchies have no doubt produced a long and mostly unwritten history of wife battering. The essential aspect of social relations deriving from these interactions, which allows for the possibility of male violence towards females, is the power differential between the genders. These gendered power differentials allow men unwarranted power in relation to women. Furthermore the patriarchal mobilisation of bias actively supports a husband's practical privileges should he batter his wife. Specific structures deriving from capitalism have enhanced and helped entrench patriarchal privileges which are conducive to male violence against females. The public–domestic split as we know it is one of these structures.

The public–domestic societal division separates men from women on a mass scale and perpetuates the patriarchal power relations. This does not mean that this division causes violence by men against women, but it may add to the foundations which allow the possibility of such violence. Separations deriving from the public–private split emphasise the difference between the two genders. Difference, in combination with perceived limited resources, can provoke the expression of violence. Grouped males, because of our society's patriarchal biases, can label the others—females in another work section or at home—as inferior, less important, unskilled.

Eli Zaretsky contends that our domestic–public societal split is neither universal, biologically based nor ahistorical: it is a socially constructed class-related division arising from nineteenth century capitalism. The proletarianisation of the free, individual, industrial worker uprooted him from his domestic and feudal social matrices. 'The family became the major sphere of society in which the individual could be foremost—it was the only space that proletarians "owned". Within it, a new sphere of social activity began to take shape.'[21] The individual 'owner' referred to here is of course male. The worker in the capitalist mode of production is doubly split. He does not work where he lives, and his emotional and social needs are difficult to fulfil in the public domain. The worker has the potential to utilise his own labour power but he has little control over when, where, how or by whom this potential will be used. He does not own his time or the products of his labour.

Men have attempted to compensate for this diminished autonomy by organising guilds and other work-related associations. Heidi Hartmann considers these male activities had dire consequences for female participation in the wage-labour market.

> Since men acted in the political arena as heads of households and in the households as heads of production units it seems likely that they would develop more organisational structures beyond their households...Men's organisational knowledge, then, grew out of their position in the family and in the division of labour.[22]

Patriarchal relations and the domination of unions by men have meant that from a labour relations perspective women have been excluded, rather than organised.[23] Thus working men have retained some power in the public domain.

A consequence of these historical circumstances is that women have very little power in the public domain deriving from either the family or wage-labour. As Eisenstein states

> ...because women were often given and were not the givers, because they had no control over the arrangements surrounding their lives... [they] came to experience the exchange system as a system of relations which excluded them from decisions, purposive activity, and control.[24]

Thus, during industrialisation, men lost work autonomy and gained some power in the private domain; women lost some public voice and took up new domestic responsibilities.

'Material production within the family—the work of housewives and mothers—was devalued since it was no longer seen as integral to the production of commodities.'[25] Women increasingly lost direct participation in work (public) activities and their social networks were also disrupted. Furthermore they became more responsible for the emotional support of the male worker who spent most of his day surviving the demands of the industrial workplace. Women's responsibilities towards the children also increased because the workers out in the public domain were not at home to contribute to child raising. Thus women gained a different sort of work load which involved increased responsibilities and lost the companionship and status which had been associated with the private domain as a centre of production of goods for exchange.

Zaretsky summarises the post-industrial creation of the position and responsibilities of a housewife in the following way.

> The newly emerged areas of personal life were the housewife's responsibility—in particular childhood, but also sexuality, emotional expression...Far from being a refuge for women the family was a workplace...[and] neither women nor children had any private space within the home.[26]

No matter how far back this goes, the wife as nurturer of the husband is relevant to wife battering.

> Women are nurturers and caretakers. Men expect this and when something bad happens, men blame women for it. If she can't figure it out, she isn't doing her job and *she* is hurting me...If she loves me, she will understand me. If she doesn't understand, she's not doing her job; she's a *bad* wife.[27] (First emphasis mine)

Zaretsky makes clear that emotional and personal replenishment of the male worker is an extra responsibility for the worker's wife in the domestic domain. As he has little control over his labouring, so she has little control over this aspect of her work in that she cannot alter the structures and practices at his workplace, but she has the brief of dealing with his overall emotional wellbeing.

The present day public–domestic schism affects the possibility of male violence towards wives in a number of ways. Firstly the separation of males off into the world of work may provide a male support network. In some Mediteranean countries, the visibility of males in the public arena—for example, the plaza or cafe—even when they are not working gives further credence to the notion that the separate location offers a refuge to men and provides mutual support. There is at least one study of male perpetrators of violence against women which implicates frequent contact with male peers as a factor increasing the likelihood of the continuance of the violence.[28] The resistance of male workers to women entering previously 'male' places of work may also be related to a sense of solidarity that men may experience in the workplace.

Secondly, as the separation of men in the public domain and women in the domestic domain enhances the potential for male networking, so it diminishes the potential for female congregations. Workplaces (for paid employment) comprise numbers of workers, but the home—the site of unpaid employment—usually consists of one worker and some dependent children. Child care and housework in our present society are time-consuming activities. Thus the times in which women can leave their individual settings and meet with each other are limited and often such gatherings—for example, playgroup—are child focused and do not free up the mothers much at all. 'After-hours' gatherings are also circumscribed by further household work.

The public–domestic divisions as we know them underpin the isolation of the home from the 'world of work' and the isolation of women from each other. Given patriarchal power relations, husbands may determine their wives activities whilst they are at home and when they are not. The old saying, 'a man's home is his castle', gives support to this. Clearly the king is in charge of the castle whether he is there or not, and some kings determine the course of events in greater detail than others. Thus if the husband is in charge at home, and home is separated from the rest of society, then the husband is free to exercise his comparative power advantage however he chooses.

If the husband chooses to exploit his position of power vis-à-vis his wife by using violence against her, she has minimal resources with which to protect herself in that environment. And certainly most wife battering takes place at home rather than in public places. Hence the irony is that the domestic domain by definition devolves on mothers and children but the home is not necessarily the woman's castle. Some battering men determine the hourly activities of their wives whilst they are out 'at work' by detailing the how, when and where of the chores of the day. Many battering men recognise the isolation of women as an advantage to themselves by forbidding and breaking up friendships and sundering the relations of their wives with their family of origin. Thus the public–domestic divisions in our society are not innocent structures when husbands batter wives, but decrease the likelihood of females gathering resources to escape the violence.

During these changes in capitalist societies in the nineteenth and twentieth centuries, the proletarianised male labourer lost some public power and regrouped along union lines fighting for male rights in the workplace.

Concomitantly, male employers—the bourgeoisie—and their upper middle class representatives gained power and control over large numbers of workers. These male members of the bourgeoisie, by virtue of their wealth in terms of capital and access to labour, wielded increased power in the social and ideological domains. Thus in all major aspects of the public sphere men—bourgeois men—came to hold positions of power. Patriarchal premises devolving on gendered power relations, therefore, were built into the material, economic and emotional social structure. The public sphere and bourgeois male power coincided. The domestic sphere became synonymous with individualised 'non-productive' females and children. Women may have some autonomy at home, but as far as worldly influence goes the domestic sphere is 'subsumed' by the public sphere.[29] These changes, of course, were not absolute.

However, overall, women lost the power to influence the workplace, were relegated to the inferior status of housewife, were split off from other workers of their kind and gained complex and nebulous responsibilities which were difficult to fulfil.

THE STATE AND INSTITUTIONALISED VIOLENCE

In the public sphere (including the state), men determine such things as policies, economic practices, laws, religious dogma, educational methods and goals, social mores, media content, scientific principles, war protocols, international relations, research directions and trends in music, art and literature. The acceptability or otherwise of violence is determined by male policymakers directly and indirectly. There are written and unwritten codes with regard to who can behave violently towards whom, under what circumstances, utilising which methods. As well as individual and group codes, males in positions of public power determine international and national levels of 'acceptable' violence and what types of violence become institutionalised in the workplace and within families. As Murray Straus says:

> The necessity for and efficacy of much governmental violence is highly questionable as illustrated by the controversy over the efficacy of the death penalty, of police toughness, and of the still widespread practice of physical punishment in the schools...Finally there is the fact that our government [the USA] maintains a world-wide military establishment. These examples of governmental violence provide powerful models for the behaviour of individual citizens. They form an important part of an even more general normative system, which holds that violence can and should be used to attain socially desirable ends.[30]

The issue that Straus does not mention in the exegesis above is that military personnel, the police, executioners and even school principals are predominantly male. Thus it is *male* violence at the individual and international levels that is made policy and implemented.

Violence in our society, as well as being institutionalised and legitimised, is deemed to be news, entertainment and exciting. Newspapers, television programmes, magazines, books, movies, videos, pornography and plays—as well as opera[31] and poetry to a lesser extent—contain a high level of violence. Again the majority of this material is written, produced, directed, photographed and acted by males.

> Violence in the mass media both reflects the existing high level of aggression and violence in American society and helps perpetuate that pattern. The typical citizen watches 'prime time' T.V. in which more than half of all characters are involved in some violence, including one out of ten in killing.[32]

Thus violence in some form is in everybody's house on a daily basis. This violence is mostly perpetrated by males. Males with public power also determine whether men may behave violently towards women, whether only some men can, whether they can under specified circumstances or whether only some women in specific situations are 'acceptable' targets. Army and police personnel and violent movie stars are usually men, and their victims are also usually men. However we do see army violence towards 'foreign' women, police violence towards women who take 'unacceptable' public stands, and the movie 'heroes' may treat women like servants and sex objects and occasionally 'rough up' a co-star who behaves 'inappropriately'.

Male policymakers also determine 'acceptable' levels of violence against women in general. Feminists see this violence as an integral aspect of patriarchy and the social control of women. Force and its threat is the ultimate sanction men may use against women, given the power differences between the two sexes within and outside marriage. Awareness of the possibility of rape or assault perpetrated by some men against some women has the effect of confining the activities of women and rendering them in awe of unknown men as potential attackers and known men as possible protectors. Jalna Hanmer highlights the insidious social control mechanisms deriving from women's awareness of men's violence.

> In a woman's life fear of violence from men is subtle and pervasive. At a subliminal level, fear is experienced as unease, a concern to behave properly...Fear can be activated by knowledge of actual violence to oneself, to known or unknown others, or by deviating from accepted social behaviour or even contemplating doing so. What deters one woman may not deter another.[33]

Over the centuries, males in the public sphere have also determined whether male violence towards specific women—namely wives—is acceptable. Thomas Aquinas deemed that men had the right to beat their wives as long as they did not murder them. Later the public Protestant position was that 'husbands were counselled to be kind and considerate to their wives, to refrain from criticising them publicly and to chastise them with moderation'.[34] Presumably this level of 'chastisement' was somewhat less than near murder and was therefore a decrease in the acceptable extent of violence that a husband could mete out to his wife.

Straus, making a more contemporary comment, views the marriage licence as a 'hitting licence'. He acknowledges that 'this is so much a taken for granted, unperceived, unverbalised norm, [and] so contrary to the way most of us view marriage'.[35] It is not, perhaps, that the marriage licence specifically allows or encourages husbands to be violent towards wives, but that if a husband does assault his wife the law frequently does not act as if this is a criminal act. Thus the marriage licence, because of the patriarchal biases built into the law, actually protects a husband who is violent towards his wife and it does not offer *her* any protection at all.

Catholicism and Protestantism both have a history of acceptance of husband violence. Straus notes that such beliefs have permeated the 'male-oriented organization of the criminal justice system [which] virtually guarantees that few women will be able to secure legal relief'.[36] Men holding public positions of power have actively and passively condoned the principle that husbands may beat their wives; and if they do the law will not seriously and assiduously sanction against such violence.

Jocelyn Scutt considers that the law is permeated by patriarchal beliefs and practices.

> Patriarchal values are not only reflected in courts of criminal law.
> They provide foundations for the family jurisdiction. Judges,
> counsellors, and lawyers working through the Family Court of
> Australia have been trained, like criminal law lawyers, magistrates,
> and judges, in law schools steeped in the ancient regime of woman as
> property, woman as secondary to man.[37]

The patriarchal nature of the law is by no means impregnable. Social facts, such as 25 per cent of all murders in New South Wales are spouse killings[38], are sometimes acknowledged publicly. The Crimes (Domestic Violence) Amendment Act NSW came into effect in April 1983. This legislation intends to achieve three purposes:

- it clarifies the power of the police to enter private premises where a domestic violence offence is occuring or is suspected to have occurred;
- it makes a spouse a compellable witness in prosecutions for domestic violence, thus removing the previous 'choice' which could exacerbate revenge tendencies of the aggressor spouse;
- it establishes a procedure whereby a person who fears violence, molestation or harassment may obtain an apprehended domestic violence order imposing restrictions on the aggressor spouse's behaviour for up to six months. The order is available to *de jure* or *de facto* spouses whether they are currently cohabiting or not.[39]

Such legislation is a start. So are male-run men's groups which exist in nascent form in Australia to discuss such topics as their concerns about sexual practices, controlling behaviours and alcohol consumption, with a view to increasing their own level of insight into patriarchal practices which are problematic to them. The aim for many men who establish and contribute to such groups is to change a range of behaviours which they (or sometimes their women partners) feel uncomfortable about or critical of. These men, although small in number, are swimming against powerful patriarchal currents in unknown waters. As with the majority of women who joined the Australian women's movement some 25 years ago, very few have successful role models from the previous generation to draw upon.

In the United States there are large numbers of men who work with problem men. The well-known groups such as RAVEN (Rape and Violence End Now) and EMERGE (a Men's Counselling Service for Domestic Violence Perpetrators) engage in political demonstrations, lobbying and public education programmes as well as crisis intervention and short- and long-term counselling. Some Australian feminists seem to be very critical of these organisations and fear that the new-found (more authentic) male solidarity may also have anti-female consequences. No doubt some women's groups have anti-male consequences. I believe Harry Brod to be sincere when he declares that the most dynamic aspect of the American men's movement is its commitment to nonviolence. After all, men en masse have more to lose by institutionalised rampant violence in our society than women—they get killed in wars, deal with male violence as police, etc.

Men's studies by and large view individual male perpetrators of violence as '*over* conformists, men who have responded all too fully to a particular aspect of male socialization'.[40] Such men are looking for male socialization as a source of violence and find much evidence of this, from acceptance of male fights within the family and schoolyard, to gangs, sports and other male-versus-male competitive activities. Hence male violence at the individual and macro levels is being scrutinised and criticised; and mechanisms to strengthen male resistance to these powerful institutionalised imperatives are being activated.

PATRIARCHAL PROFESSIONS

In New South Wales in 1983 the law acknowledged the existence of spousal violence, deemed it unacceptable and provided a framework for protecting the victim and prosecuting the attacker. However, three-and-a-half years later, a policy adviser on domestic violence with the New South Wales Police Department made the comment that the police had 'not yet totally embraced the legislation'. A police sergeant put this into clearer perspective.

> There is some resistance from police, but there is also resistance from sectors of the judiciary. A lot of police are discouraged by the lack of support from the system, and this ultimately reinforces their belief that domestic violence is a family matter.[41]

Thus there is police and judicial resistance to the implementation of the Crimes (Domestic Violence) Act.[42] Nevertheless, the police in New South Wales in 1986 were making a concerted effort to improve the police response to domestic violence in metropolitan and country regions. This effort will need to be sustained to make the Domestic Violence Act as useful in reality as it looks on paper.

After a study of 24,428 domestic disputes in Ohio, Daniel Bell concluded that 'the police have failed to make arrests in domestic dispute and violent incidents when they were legally justified to do so'.[43]

According to Scutt, before the Domestic Violence Act was proclaimed, the police had the right, even the duty, to intervene when a spouse was beaten.

> At common law, police in Australia are under an obligation to protect life and property...There is no adequate reason for failing to include within the obligation to protect, persons who are married to their assailants, or persons who are cohabiting with their attackers.[44]

Police claim that husbands charged with assault of their wives are infrequently convicted and/or given a minimum fine which deems their intervention and arrest a waste of time. This may well be their justification for their inaction, based on their patriarchal views about men, women and marriage. A 1981 (American) study was carried out by Lawrence Sherman and Richard Berk on 314 police interventions in cases of spousal assault in which the assaulter was randomly arrested, given advice or ordered to leave the home for eight hours. This project revealed that official follow-up and victim report data six months later showed that the arrested suspects manifested significantly less subsequent violence than those who were ordered to leave or given advice.[45]

This shows that patriarchal beliefs of individual police officers and lawyers can be accessed and changed to some extent. Of course belief change is not enough to deal with violent men. The Sherman and Berk study reveals that teaching police officers basic conflict resolution skills, and empowering them to fulfil the letter of the law in such instances, has an impact on violence perpetrators. However individuals in positions of power within the Police Force have to have a strong commitment to positive change, and the money, time and labour power to access larger numbers of police workers in order to raise their consciousness of the issues, inform them of their responsibilities and provide them with some skills and confidence to deal with tense and dangerous domestic disputes.

As with members of the legal profession and the police, general practitioners and accident and emergency department health workers also deal with wives who have been battered by their husbands, and less so with the batterers themselves. Battered women's injuries are frequently severe enough to warrant attention in a hospital or a general practitioner's surgery. The majority of medical responses to battered women are to deal with the injuries, ignore the events surrounding the violence and avoid even a referral. When the 'patient' repeatedly enters the medical domain, she is highly likely to be prescribed minor tranquillisers or analgesics[46], as well as stitches and topical medication appropriate for the injuries. An American College of Physicians (1986) paper recommends that physicians refer battered women to social workers and mental health workers.[47]

According to Evan Stark, Anne Flitcraft and William Frazier, most battered women are not even 'recognized' by the medical profession as victims of their husband's violence. Even when they are recognised it seems that treating the victim as if she were sick is the first line of response. More appropriate referrals would be to a women's refuge, a domestic violence hot line or a female worker at the more generic community health centre. Again, it seems that the male-dominated professions are imbued with patriarchal values and fail to deal effectively with female victims of spouse abuse. What Scutt says of police officers could also be applied to members of other male-dominated professions.

Police officers are expected not to be influenced by their personal lives in dealings with the public and treatment of crime. Whether male or female, whether married or not, whether they beat their own wives (or husbands), law enforcement officers have a duty to uphold the law. Their duty is to protect people and property.[48]

This is a call for professionals to adhere to objective professional standards. From the literature on wife battering, it is clear that this particular area of professional practice is difficult to deal with compassionately and effectively unless specific in-service training is offered and required to be undertaken. If patriarchal beliefs about the rights of a man within marriage impede professional capabilities, they must be an intrinsic aspect of their personal beliefs as well.

Perhaps such questionnaires as those used by Rodney Stark and James McEvoy (1970) and Straus (1974) to ascertain representative views of the rights of husbands to be physically violent towards their wives actually under-represent the proportion of the male population who hold such views. If men in professional positions of authority believe that husband to wife violence is unacceptable, it would seem that they would be likely to convey this attitude and/or state it. Such is not the case. If we leave aside the professions and ask men generally if they would state their disapproval of violence to a husband who revealed he had been violent towards his wife, what percentage would answer in the affirmative? Eighty per cent? That is approximately the percentage of the public who do not approve of hitting a wife under any circumstances.[49] Not approving does not equal disapproval. This is no doubt one of the reasons why lawyers, doctors and ministers of religion do not often show professional disapproval of wife battering. The targeting of young police officers may indicate that such an occupation is more amenable than the higher status professions to having their beliefs questioned and practices changed!

THE PATRIARCHAL LABOUR MARKET—WELFARE—TAX NEXUS

Beliefs and practices in the male-dominated professions can be seen to have patriarchal underpinnings. In this country, in this century, the area of social legislation is also predicated on the patriarchal relations between men and women and the responsibility of women to raise children. These relations are not made explicit by policymakers but the effects of social legislation are such that the public–private division has been built into the foundations of much policymaking. Bettina Cass states that the conventional division of labour regarding child care is assumed in family and welfare policies, that is, it is expected that it will be the woman's income which will be foregone on the birth of a child. That mothers are most financially disadvantaged by childbirth and child rearing is not explicitly acknowledged. The financial recompense by the state for this disadvantage is couched in terms of compensation for 'parents' and the transfer of payments to the 'household'.[50] Thus the financial constraints imposed on women in comparison to men within a family which is raising children are not acknowledged. The family unit implies a unity of interests, but this is not necessarily so[51], and women's financial needs in contrast to family financial needs are not addressed.

Straus pinpoints the patriarchal assumptions informing the notion of parenting in our society.

> The most fundamental policy implication. . .has to do with the sexual stereotyping of parental responsibilities. Under the present system, a husband does not need to fear that if he beats his wife and she leaves, *he* will be responsible for both the care of the child and the need to earn sufficient income.[52]

At the present time in Australia, the male wage is no longer structured to allow any man on a lower salary scale to support a wife and two or three children. As well, the family allowance is paid at a flat rate until combined parental income is $50,000 per annum. This means that in poor families the male wage earner may not earn enough money to maintain his wife and family, even though the social expectation that he should do so may still be the norm. The family allowance is so paltry that it does not bridge the gap. As the man is in a contradictory position, so is the woman—the social expectation may be that she should stay home and raise the children. How can she do that if there is not enough money to feed them? Hence the two-income family (or one plus one-third incomes), provided that both the husband and wife are able to find employment.[53]

These financial strictures and social contradictions do not cause husbands to be violent towards wives, but add to the practical survival stresses of families on low incomes. Studies repeatedly show that there are greater rates of violence towards wives in lower socioeconomic classes, and the fact that such data may be class biased need not decrease the level of domestic violence in those classes. Some studies reveal that unemployed husbands behave more violently towards their wives than employed husbands. This may not be surprising in that unemployment or low male wages not only make survival for the whole family more difficult, but also decrease the husband's access to a range of material resources, his ability to wield power and his access to the public domain.

Some writers believe that since the 1960s individual families in Western countries have maintained their children overall by the increased labour participation of married women.[54] According to Margaret Wynn, 'employed women have done more in the post-war period to augment the income, and hence the welfare, of their families than any cash transfer or tax benefit provided by governments'.[55] These financial contributions made by women are rarely acknowledged: the opportunities for women to earn an income are less than those for men, and continuity of employment is virtually impossible due to the likelihood that the mother will carry out most of the parenting tasks during the early childhood years. The incomes of female workers who are out of the workforce raising children for some years are likely to resemble those of the less skilled male worker. Peak income will be lower and early, and if she can re-enter the workforce later, the salary is likely to be less than the earlier peak[56] and remain at such a plateau with few accrued benefits.

In 1989 the average weekly total earnings of all women was 65 per cent of the average for men.[57] Thus the patriarchal structure of the labour market supports male material advantages inside and outside the family. This forces the economic dependence of women, increases men's resentment and decreases women's potential for economic independence either to ameliorate family difficulties or to establish a separate economic unit.

As the patriarchal division of labour has been assumed by social legislators, then women who are married and are mothers are generally economically dependent on their husbands. For person A to wield power over person B, A must have some sanctions at his disposal to utilise if person B resists. In our society we need money to sustain life. If our society is structured around men working in the public domain for money and with women working in the private domain without direct payment, then husbands have significant sanctions to use in relation to their wives. According to Richard Gelles, lack of money to provide basic food and shelter is one of the three major factors associated with a wife remaining with a violent husband.[58] Furthermore, within marriage, batterers tend to be very controlling of money as well as other aspects of their wives' lives: 'violent husbands generally handle all the money; sometimes they even [sic] do the grocery shopping themselves'.[59] Within the marriage men have the power to limit women's access to money. This can have dire consequences if there is insufficient money for food or the woman has no means of escape.

Overall, the wage system, the social security system and the tax system have institutionalised the financial dependency of most wives and children on husbands and fathers. For women who experience violence at the hands of their husband and want to leave him, this means that they will have no money of their own and insufficient to maintain children unless they can get an adequately paid job. These structures impose hardships on husbands and fathers too. However, men can abrogate these responsibilities and the state will minimally support women and children in families that are not 'intact'. So ultimately the responsibility for the support of children, as Straus indicates, will fall to mothers who have difficulty in gaining access to child care facilities and paid employment.

When we look at who gains from provisions of the social welfare and fiscal welfare systems, we also need to look at who does not gain from these provisions. When we consider state legislative effects on women, children and men, we need to consider all aspects of the system; not only those that claim to impinge on specific groups, but those that at first sight may not seem to. Thus such things as population policy, taxes and industrial relations have ramifications for social welfare recipients, women, children and men. In this, no person is an island. '[The] Welfare State is not just a set of services, it is also a set of ideas about society, about the family, and—not least important—about women'.[60] These implicit beliefs about women, children and men, as well as others about class and race, become part of the infrastructure of state policies. Such unarticulated ideas are largely patriarchal. They are often not spelled out because they are assumptions which are not reflected upon by policymakers at the highest levels of government.

In general, state agencies relate to married women through their husbands, especially via the income tax and social security systems[61], and 95 per cent of women are married for at least some period of their lives.[62] If we consider Australian pensions, benefits and allowances, we can determine the veracity of the above claim. Unemployment benefits are effectively contingent on male unemployment. To receive the benefit, the combined incomes of the married couple are means-tested. If a married woman is unemployed, but her husband's income is such that they are ineligible, she cannot receive the dole in her own right. Furthermore, if the couple are eligible for the benefit, the person who applies is the recipient of the cheque. In marriages involving a battering male, he will invariably be in charge of finances, and he will be the applicant and the recipient of their combined benefit.[63] State agencies also relate to women vis-à-vis their children as much as they do via their husbands.[64] The maternity allowance, child endowment and family allowance are all paid directly to women by virtue of them bearing and raising children.

The supporting parent benefit is paid to sole supporting parents. This benefit is paid by virtue of the adult raising children but these child raisers are characterised by the absence of a spouse. That this benefit (or the supporting mother's benefit) did not come into existence until 1973, shows that marriage (or absence of it) in this instance was more pertinent to the state than the fact that sole parents were actually rearing children. Mary McIntosh summarises the contradictory impact the patriarchal social security system has on women's lives.

> In the case of women the social security system has worked in a curious way, on the one hand to establish married women as dependent upon their husbands (and therefore as not entirely reliant upon wage labour) but on the other hand by restricting their direct eligibility for social security benefits, to make them more vulnerable to use as cheap labour power when they do have to engage in wage labour.[65]

Thus there are complex relationships between the welfare state, capitalist production and marital relations.

2 | The contributions of the modern family to male violence

> All women become like their mothers. That is their tragedy.
> No man does. That's his.
>
> Algernon, *The Importance of Being Ernest*, Oscar Wilde

To properly construct a theory of the family, Mark Poster believes there must be three levels of analysis:

- the psychological;
- studies of their everyday life;
- the relation of the family to society.[1]

Poster claims that four 'ideal type' family structures can be gleaned from European history: the aristocratic and peasant families of sixteenth and seventeenth centuries, the working-class family of the early industrial revolution and the 'bourgeois' family of the mid-nineteenth century. The bourgeois model is not confined to the bourgeoisie, the model pertains to working class and middle class families. This model is especially fruitful as it existed in upper middle class Vienna at the end of last century, thus it is the milieu of Freud's studies of intra-psychic structures. These are still with us experientially and ideologically. This bourgeois family is my working model, but I will call it the modern family.

'[The] bourgeois home...divorced itself from external authority...The power of parents over children rose considerably as other authority figures in the community lost the ability to intervene in family relations'.[2] From the early nineteenth century, state legislation intruded on some working-class families but bourgeois and middle-class families remained exempt.

Thus, in the period of industrialisation in western countries, the

33

family has lost its acknowledged and actual roles in the organisation of the economy and politics. These domains, which are the engines of our society, have been radically separated from the domestic arena and run on public arena tracks. This means that men and women formerly made direct contributions to the production of goods at home, but this is now a workplace prerogative. Likewise, politics were a local and practical affair, but now the channels of influence between voter and policymaking are very tenuous.

These factors separate classes too. It is the ruling class and their middle-class representatives who make big economic and political decisions. It is not the members of the ordinary family. The fact that Poster considers power in the modern family to be a key issue is likely to be related to the loss of economic and political power. Hence the modern family is marked out as the arena in which adults can have control, make decisions and wield influence. Such autonomy is meagre against the background of gross national product, income tax policy and who will be supported in overseas wars, but this is what we have.

The patriarchal beliefs and practices which have a history prior to the public–domestic split have remained as much within the modern family as they have in the running of governments. Therefore it will not come as a surprise to realise that the power lost to men by and large in the public arena has been transposed (and whittled down) to the privacy of the modern family. This is one reason that the privacy of the 'family' is heatedly defended.

Michael Bittman has blown the whistle on the myth of equal partners in marriage in this regard. He asks the question: 'Can familial relations be based on reconstructed pre-industrial patterns of authority and yet be committed to the bourgeois ideals which inspire effective individualism?'[3] To answer that question in the affirmative we need to look below surface appearances, listen hard to couple conversations, observe interactions and document practices. These gendered power inequalities, in an era of proclaimed equality, hide themselves in mysterious superficialities, but manifest themselves in clear and concrete practices.

> . . . within a supposed symmetrical marital relation, where both partners meet as social equals, each autonomously seeking to maximize their happiness, the husband must nevertheless issue authoritative commands. Clearly this cannot be regularly done at the explicit level, so it takes the form of a metacommunicative marker.[4]

Unequal power relations under these complex circumstances are revealed by a tone of voice, a nod, leaving the room, making a comment or asking an innocent question. Bittman gives the question 'Where is my tie?' as an example. Such a question may in fact be an instruction or an accusation. If one were to ask 'Where is my bra?', do the same instructional consequences of the husband rummaging ever so speedily, efficiently and quietly through the drawers, come to mind? It is likely that women, men and children have made gains *and* losses within this family type over generations. Nevertheless Poster's point is that with these

> new forms of love and authority, the bourgeois family generated a new emotional structure...What made the bourgeois structure so unique for the child was [that] the ambivalent pulls of body and parental love were so absolute...Parental authority was absolute for the child and *equally* parental love was deep.[5]

The family is the place were virtually all of the children's emotional needs are to be satisfied and most of the spouses' emotional needs. The restriction of love choices for the child to two or often one parent means that affection is at a premium and scarce, so the child opts for love and represses his/her other needs. The double bind in relation to the child's needs versus limited affection is very significant for the children. With its concomitant economy of affection it is also significant for adults who are thrown into each others emotional, economic, practical and social arms. 'Generational and sexual conflict must be captured and understood in the same way as conflicts of class, race and religion'.[6]

Thus conflict is an integral aspect of family and social relations. Poster is one of the few family theorists writing over a decade ago who had the honesty to proclaim this state of affairs. As the power relations between men and women are often convoluted and denied, so is the fact that our daily lives are permeated by conflict in some form or other. In a society of 'individuals', conflict is inevitable. In a family of individuals with different needs and with children at various levels of development, again conflict of interest is part of the family fabric. Conflict is therefore 'normal' in our society and within our families.

Three major issues underpin Poster's understanding of the modern family which differentiates it from other family forms. These are intensity of emotional bonds due to the separation of the family from the public domain; power inequalities between parents and children as well as gendered power relations deriving from ongoing patriarchal relations; and conflict between individuals relating to the emotional intensity, the public domestic split and privacy. Poster's general definition of the family is

> The place were psychic structure is formed and where experience is characterized in the first instance by emotional patterns...the social space where generations confront each other directly and where the two sexes define their differences and power relations.[7]

Denial of the intrinsic levels of conflict in the modern family has no doubt contributed to people not having well developed constructive conflict resolution skills. With inadequate skills to deal with these difficulties, spousal conflicts and parent–child conflicts may lead to the use of violence as a tactic. Thus this modern family, with a combination of smallness, emotional intensity and concentrated parental authority, is conducive to conflict with high emotional stakes and a limited number of persons available to mediate. In combination with a dearth of constructive methods to deal with conflicts of interest, the potential for violence is immanent.

FAMILY PRIVACY—MARITAL ROLES

With the industrial revolution, the family and the home became more private and associated with women and children and disassociated from mass production and wage-labour. These tendencies have continued to intensify over the last century. This isolation augurs poorly for those residing in it. The interactions of people within the home are less visible to the public, particularly since this privacy has become sanctified over time. As Peter Laslett says, 'Since social control and observability are positively correlated, what happens within the family unit is private and therefore less subject to accountability to others'.[8] Therefore violence in the home is not necessarily observed by others, and even if it is, the contemporary majority belief is that others do not have the right to intervene or express disapproval.

The Dobashes' article on 'charivari' makes this point. In the middle ages, community members would gather their pots and pans and march, reciting homespun and barbed rhymes, to the house in which a social offender lived. There they would clang and sing out their disapproval for some time and then march on. The Dobashes believe that the practice of charivari was used to shame 'excessive' wife beaters as 'moderate' wife beating was, to a large extent, acceptable during those centuries. Charivari faded out at the end of the eighteenth century as abstract justice phased in.[9] Now, who is it in the community who is clearly saying to the violent male, 'this behaviour is unacceptable'?

The right of family privacy has been rigorously protected in legal, medical, religious and social spheres. Police are often averse to promptly attending 'domestics' not only because they are aware of the possibility that they will be hurt but because they believe domestic violence is a private activity even when legislation states otherwise. Jan Pahl highlights the fact that

> ...privacy is not an absolute value, that some people's privacy appears to be more inviolate than other people's privacy, and that by looking at how 'the private' is defined and maintained we can understand a great deal about the nature of power relations in a particular society.[10]

Of course the power relations in our society are gendered, therefore within the family the husband's right to privacy—at the legal level and often at a personal level—is greater than his wife's right to privacy.

> Ideas about marriage and the family are inextricably linked, at least in Western European thought, with ideas about privacy, and an emphasis on 'protecting privacy' can work to the detriment of those who are weakest within the social and physical space defined as private.[11]

The privacy of 'the family' under these circumstances can mean both the right of the husband to criminally assault his wife and the right of the professionals and neighbours to turn the other cheek.

Because the home is sacrosanct, David Gil considers it is safer for a family member to be violent in that setting in comparison to all others. Furthermore, frustrations arising elsewhere with other people may well be acted out in this safe environment. 'Individuals will frequently discharge violent feelings and impulses in the informal setting of their families, rather than in more formal settings where these feelings often originate'.[12] In this way the sanctity of the home can have a safety valve effect for manageable industrial relations. Disputes which arise at work but are not, or cannot, be settled there can be re-enacted overtly or indirectly at home. Zaretsky claims that it is women's work to restore the wellbeing of the man in the workforce. Therefore we might conclude that Gil's carefully non-gendered statement means that wives will bear the displaced frustrations and aggressions that men bring home, wittingly or unwittingly.[13]

Straus discusses other family characteristics which may contribute to violence within the family. After working and school hours, the family may spend a lot of unstructured time together. Family members have a broad range of activities and interests, thus there are many conflicting needs and hopes amongst individuals or family sub-groups. He recognises the intensity of emotions within the family as a significant factor. 'The failure of a work colleague to spell or to eat properly may be mildly annoying...But if the bad spelling or table manners are those of one's child or spouse, the pain experienced is often excruciating'.[14]

Within the family there are many impinging activities which have to be chosen between, for example, in one room with one television set, two programmes cannot be watched simultaneously. He also considers that 'membership in a family carries with it an implicit right to influence the behaviour of others'.[15] This entitlement leads to much more interference in the activities of others within the family than without. The age range, and the fact that most families contain both genders, incorporates a range of subcultures under one roof. The ascribed roles deriving from patriarchal family prescriptions are bound to be challenged by children on the one hand and at least the female spouse. Straus also recognises family privacy as having a hothouse effect. Overall he considers family membership to be involuntary—obviously so for the children, but often pragmatically so for either spouse—and leaving is easier said than done.[16]

The role of woman as wife is one of the pre-eminent views of women in our society.[17] (The Concise Oxford Dictionary gives the derivation of the word 'woman' as from the Old English word *wifmon* (wife, man) and wife from *wif* meaning woman. Thus woman and wife have been one, as have man and wife!) The notion that the husband is 'head' of the household is still a common belief. Thus the implication is that women should be wives, and wives should do their husband's bidding and accept whatever treatment is meted out. The position of 'head' of the family entitles the incumbent to determine what this shall mean for other family members in practice.

The second major role of women is that of mother, and the concept and practice of 'parenting' is frequently understood as 'mothering'. Within the modern family, the responsibility for child raising is assumed to be borne by the mother—these assumptions are held by employers of men and women, the tax system, the social security system, school teachers, the medical profession, relatives and friends. As parenting is a full-time-plus-overtime job and there are very few places available in childcare centres, the mother of young children is frequently forced to be 'unemployed' from a wage-labour point of view, even though she is fully occupied and has no direct access to an income. Even if she chooses to be a full-time raiser of children and housekeeper she is still not guaranteed an income or reasonable working conditions.

As Straus points out:

> ...a husband...can be reasonably confident that if she does leave, he will not have the children unless he insists on it...It is no shame for a father to claim that the child will be best off with the mother, but for a mother to assert this is not only shameful, but in many cases will cause the child to be institutionalized or placed in a foster home.[18]

The roles for women within the family do not convey a notion of power, and are very explicit and overly extensive. A woman's role as mother could be concretely interpreted as the woman doing anything that needs to be done with and for the children. The interpretation of this role in many families comes close to this extreme version. The role of mothering neatly overlaps with the woman's more general role of being responsible for the physical nourishment and emotional wellbeing of all family members. This of course can mean the woman physically and emotionally nurturing her husband. This job of feeding him, looking after him and protecting him easily overlaps with her as his servant, doing anything he will not or cannot do for himself. The third role of women in the home is that of housekeeper. As with looking after children and a husband, this too can be so comprehensive as to be never-ending. The phrase 'a woman's work is never done' is testimony to the actual impossibility of having the shopping, cooking, cleaning, washing, children's needs and husband's needs all attended to completely.

The extensive nature of the patriarchal role expectations for women in the family, in conjunction with the lack of comprehensive role expectations for men in the family, has ramifications with regard to the potential for violence by husbands towards their wives. Men can easily make many claims that their wife's work is not done. Women could perhaps claim that it is the man's fault if he does not earn enough income to maintain the family. Then given that husbands are 'head' of the household, maybe wives do not have the right to lodge a complaint! When an incident is described by a battered wife, claims are often made that a meal was too hot or late, a shirt not ironed well, her clothes not appropriate, the house too dirty, the children too noisy, or something similar. Thus capitalist-patriarchal expectations of women within the family can be extreme, rigid and unrealistic. Any woman marrying or living with a man with these expectations will inevitably fail to fulfil them and may become a target of his violence, not because she is intrinsically inadequate but because she has failed to do the impossible.

From the above description of the capitalist-patriarchal view of the family, it is clear that the role of women and expectations about women in the family are explicit whereas those with regard to men in the family are not. The two main roles attributed to men in the family are 'breadwinner' and 'head of the family'—the latter being a role which does not define activities but conveys a general notion of patriarchal authority.[19]

Straus acknowledges that

> if every man were, in fact, superior to his wife in such resources as intelligence, knowledge, occupational prestige and income there would be a concordance between ascribed authority and the individual achievements implicitly expected to accompany that authority in individual achievement-oriented societies. Clearly, that is often not the case, despite the fact that society gives men tremendous advantages in access to these traits and resources. Consequently, many men must fall back on the 'ultimate resource' of physical force to maintain their superiority.[20]

In Straus' opinion, there is a definite connection between the patriarchal expectation that a man will have more power within the family than a woman and the possibility of him using his superior physical power against her. Men (and women) have specific expectations of marital roles, but these are usually not made explicit during courtship. The expectation differences have a potential for conflict themselves.

GENDER STEREOTYPES AND MARITAL CONSEQUENCES

It is important to investigate in detail some practical aspects of stereotypical interactions between marital partners. Sociologists who investigate gender construction and reproduction need to look at what happens in families, between husband and wife, and both parents in relation to the children. These relationships are powered gender relations *par excellence*. According to Larry Feldman, sex roles are culturally defined expectations (norms) that delineate a set of 'appropriate' (expected or desirable) and 'inappropriate' (forbidden or undesirable) attitudes and behaviours for males and females.[21] After reviewing research studies on the psychological and sociological aspects of sex roles over two decades, Feldman arrived at the following prescriptive and proscriptive characteristics.[22] The most important aspect of these two lists are that the genders are dichotomous. Men are what women are not, and vice versa.

The female role

Women are expected to be (or allowed to be) the following:

1 home-oriented, child(ren)-oriented
2 warm, affectionate, gentle, tender
3 aware of feelings of others, considerate, tactful, compassionate
4 moody, high-strung, temperamental, excitable, emotional, subjective, illogical
5 complaining, nagging
6 weak, helpless, fragile, easily emotionally hurt
7 submissive, yielding, dependent

The male role

Men are expected to be (or allowed to be) the following:

1	ambitious	10	strong	19	harsh
2	competitive	11	tough	20	severe
3	enterprising	12	powerful	21	stern
4	worldly	13	aggressive	22	cruel
5	calm	14	forceful	23	autocratic
6	stable	15	decisive	24	rigid
7	unemotional	16	dominant	25	arrogant
8	realistic	17	independent		
9	logical	18	self-reliant		

These male characteristics fall into three clusters. The pragmatic public cluster comprises items 1, 2, 3, 4, 5, 6, 8, 17 and 18. The second anti-expressive cluster consists of items 7, 9, 15, 21, 23, 24 and 25. The final cluster is conducive to violence and comprises 10, 11, 12, 13, 14, 16, 19, 20 and 22. These are the gender caricatures that permeate our culture. It is disconcerting that over one-third of the male qualities have obvious associations with the potential to be violent. It is even more disconcerting that there are no equivalent nine qualities that a male can stereotypically use to work towards discussion, tolerance or peace.

Feldman asks the question: 'What is the relationship between sex roles and family dynamics?' He derives some hypotheses from research evidence in an attempt to broach this question. His first hypothesis is that 'sex-role conditioning exerts a negative influence on marital intimacy and marital problem solving by inhibiting the development and/or expression of certain forms of behaviour in men and women'.[23] In his opinion, the difficulties in problem-solving appertain primarily to the women.

'Women. . .are highly sensitive and reactive to the interpersonal aspects of their relationship with the other. Males. . .orient themselves. . .to the impersonal task of maximizing their own earnings'.[24] Other researchers claim that wives and husbands make a similar number of rejecting statements to each other but husbands cope with these statements and offer three times as many constructive and conciliatory moves.[25] Assertiveness is a prerequisite for problem solving in conflictual situations. 'Assertive behaviour involves standing up for personal rights and expressing thoughts, feelings, and beliefs in direct, honest and appropriate ways that do not violate another person's rights.[26] Many studies of group interaction in mixed sex groups from primary school through to adult workplace groups conclude that women lead less and are generally nonassertive in such settings.

The intimacy difficulties relate primarily to the men. Many of the studies Feldman reviewed found men to be verbally and nonverbally inhibited, especially with regard to expressing feelings of love, joy, fear and sadness.[27] Clearly, if men in general cannot express one way or another even the 'positive' emotions their ability to be emotionally close to any other person—wife, child, friend—is impaired. Other studies have found that in general the intensity and frequency of emotional experiencing is lower for men than it is for women.[28] This male inability to express feelings (as exemplified by the stereotypical descriptions 'calm', 'unemotional' and 'logical') has significance with regard to violent males. It also implies a level of alienation from self which could well be a long-term consequence of capitalist separation of public from private, 'work' from home and product of labour from the worker. The inability to express feelings impedes a person's ability to communicate, empathise and be intimate. If a person experiences emotions and feelings as we inherently do, their failure to express them does not mean that the feelings will disappear. Violent men are often described as being unable to express their feelings, unable to communicate or only able to express anger. Of course difficulties in verbal communication and acceptable nonverbal communication is no justification for any kind of violence, but the latter is more likely to eventuate if other modes of expression have not been well developed. People can only develop these skills with practice, and the male stereotype mitigates against effective communication being a desirable goal.

Feldman's second hypothesis is that 'sex-role conditioning promotes the development and expression of certain dysfunctional attitudes and behaviours in men and women, and these have negative effects on marital intimacy and marital problem solving.[29] The dysfunctional behaviours of wives he focuses on are 'nagging' and 'pressuring'. Marion Meade considers that 'nagging' serves two purposes: 'the expression of serious grievances', and the 'dismemberment of the husband's ego'![30] 'Nagging' is thus the impotent expression of problems one is aware of but which one believes one can do nothing about. It is also annoying to the person who is the target of the 'nagging'. Such behaviour, because it is nonassertive, cannot produce positive change. As with 'nagging', 'emotional pressuring' is a nonconstructive sign of disssatisfaction which makes the other party of the grievance feel, personally, but non-specifically, attacked. Thus some steam is let off, but without any mutually satisfying outcome.

The dysfunctional male behaviours Feldman discusses here are passive-aggressive behaviour and physical violence. Passive-aggressive behaviours include procrastination, forgetting, avoiding direct confrontation, leaving the room during a discussion and quietly and doggedly resisting the demands of others. As with 'nagging', this behaviour is annoying to the other party. Also it is nonassertive and therefore cannot produce positive change. The avoidance and the resisting are sometimes task-specific but the issue which needs confronting is usually obscured and, if 'pressured', the person behaving passive-aggressively may not actually know what his problem is. Thus it can be seen that 'nagging' and passive-agressiveness may be complementary nonassertive behaviours which reinforce each other without ever leading to problem solving. In fact such interactions may become part of a cycle building up towards violence. The passive-aggressive person by virtue of not dealing with the issues of concern may ultimately express his dissatisfaction by being actively aggressive. By pointing out the interactional aspects of these behaviours I do not excuse a husband's violence because his wife 'nags'.

Clearly Feldman believes that male violence arises, at least to some extent, from 'normal' male characteristics encouraged by our society. In his prescriptive model, Feldman uses such words as 'tough', 'dominant', 'cruel' and 'autocratic', which have a commonsense association with the potential for violence. Feldman also acknowledges that some sectors of our society still accept that husband to wife violence is acceptable under some circumstances. Pogrebin's study of fighting in public places, when no male observer attempted to intervene while a male actor was apparently beating a woman, supports such a position.[31] As with passive-aggressiveness and other forms of indirect communication, violence produces a short-term sense of personal 'control' in those who use such methods. However none of these methods deal with whatever the problems are, therefore they remain unsolved and the communication *modus operandi* remains unchanged and the pattern is perpetuated. This is frequently the case with violent men. Should they choose another wife, the violence is highly likely to continue.

'Women are regarded as less interested in sex than men, and are expected to put limits to inappropriate masculine advances'.[32] Other studies see females as sexually passive. Behaving as a sexually passive recipient is also related to assertiveness as non-assertive people have difficulty in saying 'yes' or 'no' clearly, and certainly are not well equipped to pursue their own needs (sexual or otherwise). Men are seen as 'active, aggressive pursuers of sexual gratification from women'.[33] Here we have the passive-active complementarity in the sexual arena.[34] The aggressive pursuit of one's own needs is also nonassertive as it is characterised by demanding or taking rather than by negotiating. If the male believes that only a female can satisfy his sexual needs[35], that she should satisfy them and it is his role to see that these ends are achieved, aggressiveness is a likely outcome. Given the power differentials within marriage, men are more likely than women to determine the what, when and how of sexual activity. This is the case for the majority of modern north American couples, and there is no reason to believe that Australian women are any more in control of their sex life.[36]

Feldman is content to view the sexual issue from the stereotypical male position himself. That is, sex difficulties between heterosexual partners is primarily due to women having 'less interest in sex'. Sexual activities here seem to have acquired the narrow male meaning of genital sex. Women may have 'more interest in sex' if sex is re-defined to mean sharing affection, sensuality and genital sex. Sexual dissatisfaction between a female and male may in fact be due to male disinterest in broader sexual-sensual interactions.

According to at least one man, he would prefer to read a sexy novel whilst lying in bed next to his wife, rather that having sex with her.

'I would have to turn on the sensitivity; I would have to ask her what's been goin' on with her, what she's been dealin' with, I mean with the kids and the house, and the budget and her mom and everything like that. I'd have to tell her what was happenin' with me. My problems, my worries, I'd have to hold her, I'd have to stroke her, I would have to commit myself to an act which these days I may or may not be able to consummate. You think that is easy?'[37]

Is this a sexual difficulty: or is it some aspect of marriage which is much broader?

Marital conflict may also exhibit the same circular patterns which derive from dichotomous sex roles. One of the most common complaints that spouses have about their marriage is poor communication. Jessie Bernard claims that one marriage is really two—hers and his; so Feldman claims that 'lack of communication' has two meanings—hers and his. Women mean that men do not share their feelings and thoughts with their wives. Men mean that women complain too much and are critical. The circularity here is that the 'husband's lack of expressiveness triggers wives' over-expressiveness, which, in turn, further inhibits husband's expressiveness'.[38] Expressiveness as used by Feldman here is a nonassertive and nonconstructive expression, namely 'nagging' and 'pressuring' which the men experience as an attack and either withdraw from—the passive-aggressive response or less often resort to violence. In either case the problems are not solved and a foundation of unresolved conflict is established.

The combination of male nonexpressiveness and male sexual aggressiveness may be a potent admixture. Although words associated with violence appear in Feldman's list of 25 male characteristics, there are no adjectives relating explicitly to sexual activity. Commonsense tells me that males do believe that heterosexual (in particular) sexual activities are a part of their masculine repertoire. In some men it seems that many of their feelings are converted to anger, in others many of their feelings may be expressed sexually. Andy Metcalf, on the subject of male sexuality, writes:

> Wanting to have sex a lot, feeling a great need for it, is often quite tied up with misery. There's no direct link between feeling sexy, feeling erotic, having desire for someone else, and wanting sex . . . I think sex is a vehicle for many needs and feelings; making things better when you're feeling tense, anxious, feeling out of contact with somebody and out of contact with yourself.[39]

Here we can see indirectly that the capitalist patriarchal expectations of a wife or lover include sexual service on a variation of the nurturance theme. Expectations of women's sexual passivity is also endorsed in that a woman who does not feel like having sex at a given time under these circumstances is not merely refusing sex but is refusing to offer a range of complex emotional services.

Under these specific circumstances, female refusal of sex could be followed by violence, even though sex is not necessarily the essence of what the male needs.

EQUALITY, ASSERTIVENESS AND PROBLEM SOLVING

The main conclusion I draw from Feldman is that complementary roles have a certain clarity, but they are dehumanising for the people in the polarised roles, and they perpetuate themselves, particularly within a given relationship. Readers with an awareness of their own complexities may scorn the idea that these stereotypes have significance in our society. I consider these dichotomised stereotypes to be alive and well in Australia, across all classes. The characteristics such as fearing intimacy and being sexually aggressive are personal counterparts of ideas and practices surrounding men's work. The issues that I have raised, namely, problem-solving, intimacy, negotiation and sexual satisfaction are germane to all intimate partnerships. Given that conflict is inevitable in any present day marital set-up, it is important to realise that the complementary roles offer few problem solving possibilities. As marriage may be considered to be an arena for emotional fulfilment, it is also important to realise that the complementary roles fail to offer equitable opportunities for the giving and receiving of nurturance. I see assertiveness as a necessary but beginning characteristic for mutual emotional and sexual satisfaction as well as for problem solving.

Assertiveness skills are those required by an individual to achieve their aims in life without impinging on the rights of others or hurting others in any fashion. Nonassertive behaviours include both passive and aggressive modes of operation. Passive behaviour is self-abnegating: the actor considers their feelings, thoughts and rights to be less important than the other person's in an interactional situation. Aggressive behaviour denigrates the other person in an interactional situation; the actor believes their feelings, thoughts and rights to be more important (or the only consideration) than the other's. Passive and aggressive behaviours are complementary and in such interactions there is always a 'winner' and a 'loser'. Assertive interactions result in two respecting and respected 'winners'. Appropriate assertive negotiation can only take place when the two people concerned have *equal power*. If this is not the case the male with more power can bring external sanctions into the discussion.

Some aspects of passivity and aggressiveness will derive from unconscious relations. Others are amenable to assertive skills training and thus are amenable to change. From the preceding discussion it is clear that men who are unable to recognise or express their emotions are unable to be adequately assertive within a relationship. It is also clear that assertive resolutions require two people with such skills—one cannot guarantee successful negotiations with another passive or aggressive actor. Complementary, nonassertive interactions such as those I have discussed above are conducive to marital violence. Given the stereotypes which underpin these attempts at negotiation, it will be the male whose frustration will be expressed violently. Unlike many of the writers who use the gendered stereotypes as models, I know that this is not the whole answer. The patriarchal structures I have discussed in the previous chapter, and processes involved in gender construction covered in the next chapter, have determined the separation of 'female' and 'male' qualities, and the ways they are acted out.

The violent male is by definition nonassertive: he may be aggressive or vacillate between passivity and aggression, but by virtue of his violent transgression against another he is decidedly nonassertive in the couple context. Much of the literature on battered wives acknowledges *their* nonassertiveness. Oddly much of the information on battering husbands does not recognise this fact, although programmes for these men incorporate assertiveness skills training. Herb Goldberg, although he does not call it nonassertiveness, recognises that many males have difficulty in asking for help.

> His resistance against asking for help tends to devastate his relationships with intimates, spouse, friends, and children. If they love him, he believes, they will know what he needs...He quietly resents it when they don't. He broods in secret silence and turns himself off from them even more.[40]

And one study has shown that abusive males are significantly less assertive than nonviolent males even when the latter's marriage is conflictual.[41]

Power differences permeate spousal relations from trivial issues to serious ones. Gender stereotypes and complementary nonassertiveness are manifestations of these inequalities. Deborah McIntyre connects stereotypical interactions within the family to the use of violence by male partners.

> ...the reality of the power differential that does exist between men and women...concerns the entrenched patterns of social relations between the sexes, particularly as exhibited in the family, that are central to patriarchal society...The violence of wife beating is...the

reflection of a power struggle for the maintenance of a certain kind of social order.[42]

In this context the kind of 'problem' that the husband is trying to solve is the restoration of his power superiority *vis-à-vis* his wife. The physical violence which can occur over minor matters is generated by a struggle at this control level of the marriage. Thus violence is embedded in power structures.

> ...all violence must be seen in the context of wider power relations; it is not necessarily deviant or fundamentally different from other means of exerting power over another person. It cannot be accurately viewed as a set of isolated events, but must be placed in an entire social context.[43]

AUSTRALIAN DATA: ATTITUDES AND PRACTICES

At this stage it may be instructive to ascertain whether Feldman's dichotomous sex roles apply empirically to Australian couples. Brian English and Raymond King have analysed data from the 1976 Australian census. This information is particularly important because it derives from an adult population of 6 800 800 adults 18 years of age and over, and a sub-population of 3 164 900 practising parents. Even though the data is 14 years old, sex role differentiated attitudes and practices change slowly; and we cannot ask for a larger sample size.

The questions to be considered are gender differences in support for sex role differentiation and freedom to choose marriage, and gender differences in carrying out household tasks and child caring activities. Out of a breakdown of three categories of support—'low', 'medium' and 'high'—the category which includes the most responses from women between the ages of 18 and 39 and 50 and 54 is that of 'low' support for the sex role differentiation statements. In the remaining age groups, the most popular category for women respondents is that of 'medium' support. No female age cohort gives 'high' support for sex role differentiation. The category with the largest support from men between the ages of 18 and 34 years is that of 'low' support; but for each age cohort the percentage in this category is lower for men that it is for women. Men of 35 years and over give predominantly either 'medium' or 'high' support for the sex role differentiation statements.

The difference between the genders with regard to attitudes towards gender differentiation is notable. 'The discrepancies in support for this attitude between men and women, particularly in the age groups under 45, raise interesting questions about the number of marriages and families there are in which the partners disagree about these issues'.[44] This again raises the possibility that power issues themselves may provoke conflict within marriages. In 1976, Australian men of all ages were more supportive of men having greater authority within the marriage and in relation to child raising than were women of all ages. Patriarchal views are thus expressed by men, and presumably indicate their own expectations about their role within the family. That these expectations are not necessarily held by women sets up the potential for a disputational marital situation from the outset. The contradictions between the belief that men will be 'head' of the family and what is in store for them lay the foundation for conflict. Men with poor problem solving skills may resort to violence towards women whom they perceive as impeding their legitimate claims to authority within the family. Jerry Finn's recent study of 300 college undergraduates in the United States supports this conclusion.

> A moderately strong positive relationship was found between traditional sex role preferences and attitudes supporting the use of physical force. In addition, men were found to hold more traditional sex role attitudes than women and were more likely to endorse the use of physical force in the marital relationship.[45]

English and King's second table of interest relates to freedom to choose marriage and parenthood.[46] The category to receive the most responses from women between the ages of 18 and 34 and 45 and 49 (that is, five cohorts) is that of 'high' support (between 35 per cent and 41 per cent) for the freedom to choose marriage or parenthood. The table is divided into eleven age cohorts: amongst women, five offer predominantly 'high' support, another five offer predominantly 'medium' support and 35 per cent of the 35–39 years-of-age cohorts offer 'low' support for these choices. The category with the highest response rate from men between the ages of 18 and 59 is that of 'low' support, and men over 59 give predominantly 'medium' support for the right to choose marriage or parenthood. Again there is a striking difference between the attitudes of women and men, with the men opting for comparatively less freedom of choice with regard to these major life decisions.

As three of the items in the cluster relate to parenting rather than marriage, the views of 3 million parents should be particularly pertinent. A predominance of mothers in two-parent families (37 per cent) give support for 'low' choice, along with widowed women.[47] Not surprisingly, the never-married, separated and divorced women predominantly opt for 'high' support of choice. Overall, mothers—especially married mothers, who are the vast majority of mothers—offer little support for the freedom to choose parenthood or marriage. The category with the highest support from fathers in two-parent families (48 per cent), as well as separated and widowed men, is that of 'low' support for choice. A group of predominantly divorced fathers offer 'medium' support. No father cohorts give predominantly 'high' support for the freedom to choose parenthood or marriage. Even though the numerical majority of mothers are opting for low freedom of choice, the proportion of fathers in this category is again much larger.

When this data is analysed by the level of education of the respondents, a similar picture emerges.[48] A predominance of women who left school after 17 years of age, whether they receive further education or not, give 'high' support for the right to choose marriage or parenthood. As the qualifications increase in status the proportion of 'high' supporters increases to 67 per cent of university educated women. The numerical majority of over 1 million women who left school before the age of 15 give 'low' support, and another 1 million women who left school before the age of 17 give 'medium' support for choice.

The only cohort of men in which the majority support these choices are 39 per cent of university educated men. The majority of men who left school before 17 years of age and who have trade qualifications give 'low' support. The remaining predominance of males who left school after 17, and have technical or non-university tertiary qualifications, offer 'medium' support. Thus the numerical majority of women give 'low' or 'medium' support for choice. The numerical majority of men also give 'low' or 'medium' support. Again, though more male cohorts offer 'low' support than do female, and there are gender differences in every educational category, a greater percentage of women consistently offer 'high' support for the freedom to choose marriage or parenthood.

Again, the gender differences in the support they offer for freedom to choose marriage throughout the adult age range are significant.[49] Hence another area of conflict for men and women may be whether to marry or not, or when to do so. If men overall are less keen for freedom of choice in this arena, it indicates that they believe they are going to make some gains by marrying. Perhaps the advantages they expect are that their wives will look after them, sexually service them and provide them with children whom the women will raise. They may also expect to earn an income to financially support their spouse and children. If men and women do hold these patriarchal beliefs about marriage, it is not surprising that more women across the adult age range were supportive of being able to choose to be married or single. The only 'gain' women could perceive is to be financially supported to some extent.

Gender differences in the support for freedom to choose parenthood are also important. If men are comparatively nonsupportive of choice in this arena, what advantages are they expecting from compulsory fatherhood and motherhood? What expectations do fathers have of children whom they are overall not too willing to actively parent? This is another area of potential conflict within a marriage. Although neither of these attitudes are necessarily conducive to violence, they are indicative of a male authoritarian approach to the most important human decisions many adults make. These attitudes are underpinned by a male position of power—one cannot coerce one's equal.

As well as attitudes, English and King also investigate the practices of Australians with regard to household tasks and child raising tasks. Out of a list comprising household shopping, housework, money matters, small repairs, taking out the garbage, children's personal problems and deciding about major purchases, more than 50 per cent of parents share only the last two tasks.[50] Thus, in practice, wives and husbands see the other five tasks (irrespective of whether one or the other or both are working) as belonging to either the wife *or* the husband. This indicates that tasks within a marriage are also conceived of dichotomously, rather than to be shared by partners.

Mothers are predominantly responsible for dressing, daily care and putting children under six years of age to bed. The only task out of the four listed by English and King that the parents share is that of discipline: 48 per cent of mothers are primarily responsible and 46 per cent of the families share responsibility. Even when both of the parents work full time, discipline is still the only well shared child-centred activity. According to Michael Bittman and Frances Lovejoy, married mothers with children under 5 years of age spend almost seven times as much time performing unpaid labour than their single sisters.[51]

English and King have confirmed gender differences in attitudes and variations regarding family tasks. These gender differences are maintained for all age groups, at all educational levels, across all religious denominations, at all levels of workforce participation, whether they are parents or not, whether they are born in Australia or not and whether they are one- or two-parent families. The potential for conflict between females and males is built in attitudinally and by the practices that they report within their families. There is empirical evidence for gender differences in attitude, particularly about gender issues. There is empirical evidence for gender differences in practice, particularly in the domestic domain.

POWER, DEPENDENCY, EXPECTATIONS

The issues arising from English and King's data which relate to husband violence are power differentials, emotional and practical dependence, gender differences—both views and practices—particularly differences between the genders in regard to the desirability of sex role stereotyping.

Power relations as such are not broached by English and King. Differential power relations between women and men are an intrinsic structural aspect of our patriarchal-capitalist society. This fact has a long history and some men are cognisant of it whilst others benefit from such structural arrangements without necessarily being consciously aware of them. 'The power of a discourse resides in its hegemony, in the way it passes as truth, and in the way its premises and logic are taken for granted'.[52] The gendered power differentials exist, but women do not necessarily accept the hegemony. Such female resistance is likely to exacerbate violent tendencies in some males.

The data in English and King's study indicate that both genders see themselves as mutually dependent and therefore individually incomplete. This dependence is structurally built into dichotomous gender stereotypes in that each gender is confined to specific clusters of characteristics and skills and there is minimal overlap. Forced dependence on another person in adulthood is highly likely to cause resentments, but if each member of the dyad feels incomplete and is functionally incomplete then they are in a double bind. If either individual leaves the relationship, their only option is to find another partner to do the things they cannot do—and they are trapped again. Violence could be one *male* form of expression of frustration at this structural impasse, particularly since batterers are frequently described as conforming to rigid sex role stereotyping.

That there are significant differences in gender practices with regard to housework and child rearing is clear from English and King's data. That there are noticeable differences in beliefs about gender differences is also obvious. This divergence of interests and difference in attitudes could easily be the foundations of conflict built into the majority of relationships. These differences cross class, ethnicity, educational and age groupings. Thus if women are generally less approving of sharp gender differentiation and men are more approving, and the man in the couple relationship has more power vis-à-vis his wife, then he is in a position to attempt to force the differences he believes in or feels are important to him. One ultimate way of forcing these issues is for a husband to be violent towards a wife who seems to him to threaten some of his basic views of the world which provide him with a sense of security.

3 | The contributions of male gender construction and reproduction to male violence

> If a daughter's personality can be explained by her mother's presence, then a son's can be explained by his father's absence.
>
> Louis Nowra

In this chapter I remain within the family and investigate parenting processes in relation to the male child. Bear in mind that the family model I am using emphasises the concentration of power relations, conflict and emotional intensity. All of these interact continuously and form the terrain of parenting and growing-up. The emotional economy of the family itself is a power issue for children, because children negotiate 'choices' against a background of limited emotional resources. This of course is similar to the double bind; but affection is more basic to survival in the modern family than is the egocentric need to pursue all of one's own ends. In effect children are coerced—often without parental insight. However children recognise the flows of patriarchal power which permeate the family and adapt pragmatically to these. Such processes of negotiation for survival, self-indulgence and growth are largely unconscious, power-ridden and gendered.

To enter the unconscious domain, I utilise object relations theory which acknowledges more fully than Freud the interactive processes involved in intra-psychic childhood development. Parents are active agents (as they clearly were not deemed to be in Freud's Little Hans, for example) and they are social representatives. As the ego and super-ego of the child develop over time, elements of the active parents are negotiated internally, as are elements of the parents as embodiments of their own class, culture and history. Thus the unconscious itself—which we know

54

from historical and cultural variations within dream content—has a mediated relationship with the macro-social.

As a consequence of the above, I must begin by defining the unconscious, id, ego, superego, repression and defence mechanisms, on the grounds that these terms are not well understood. *Unconscious* processes are as important in the development of gender identity as are conscious processes. If this were not the case, we could all consciously decide to change unwanted aspects of our gender identity; and our beliefs and behaviour would coincide. As David Morgan reminds us, 'in talking about the processes of reproduction we cannot remain simply at the societal or structural level'.[1] Furthermore, 'a conception of the unconscious is essential to social theory'.[2]

INTRODUCTION TO FREUDIAN TERMINOLOGY AND OBJECT RELATIONS THEORY

At this juncture some definitions of Freudian concepts need to be stated and adhered to, particularly in relation to the 'unconscious' and 'repression' which are both often used loosely—a practice which deprives them of their significance and power. I glean the following definitions from Harold Kaplan and Benjamin Sadock's classic text.[3]

The unconscious contains repressed ideas and affects (feelings and emotions). Following *The Interpretation of Dreams*, the unconscious has the following four characteristics:

1 The *elements of the unconscious are not consciously apprehensible*. By definition, unconscious material is not conscious—it is not accessible or knowable under ordinary circumstances. Unconscious elements can only become conscious through the preconscious mind. However, one of the main functions of the preconscious is to repress emotions and traumas which the ego recognises as producing intolerable levels of anxiety. The type of mental activity associated with the preconscious is called secondary process.

2 The unconscious itself is associated with the primary process which has as its basic aim the facilitation of wish-fulfilment and instinctual drives. Hence its close connection with the pleasure principle. Primary process is not logical, it knows no negatives, it is contradictory and timeless. The language of primary process is metaphorical and *is not related to rationality or the intellect*.

3   Freud goes so far as to say that the unconscious is not verbal. However, the preconscious which mediates between the unconscious and the consciousness is closely connected with the reality principle and is verbal. Elements of the unconscious can gain access to consciousness (under limited and specific circumstances) by becoming linked with words in the preconscious. Thus the unconscious has a 'language' which is different to our common verbal currency.

4   The content of the unconscious is limited to active drives and wishes which seek satisfaction. It is not the domain of debate or constraint. These human forces are the building blocks of dreams and neurotic symptom formation. The unconscious contains the mental representatives and derivatives of intrinsic drives, especially those which are forbidden or viewed ambivalently by our society. According to Freud, two major examples are sex and aggression.

Unconscious defence mechanisms are defences utilised by the ego to keep distressing feelings unconscious and thus confine intrapsychic conflicts deriving from the oppositional nature of the id and the superego to a level that allows ego anxiety to remain tolerable. Following Freud's structural theory of the mind expounded in *The Ego and the Id* and Anna Freud's *The Ego and the Mechanisms of Defence*, I offer further definitions.

1   The id is a primordial reservoir of energy associated with the instinctual drives that demand gratification. The id is under the dominion of the primary process.

2   The ego is most easily characterised by its functions, the main ones being control and regulation of instinctual drives relating to the reality of the external world and the employment of unconscious defence mechanisms to facilitate both.

3   The superego is concerned with moral behaviour and can be seen as a social principle quite in opposition to the id. It is commonly associated with a social 'conscience' and emerges from the resolution of the oedipal complex.

Repression is a primary and *unconscious* ego defence mechanism which banishes 'unacceptable' material from consciousness. Repression is one of the basic defences available to defend the ego from disturbing anxiety. Anxiety was viewed by Freud as the ego's response to danger—actual or perceived—hence the inaccessibility of the unconscious material. It is perceived as dangerous to the ego. Repression is unknowable, unpredictable, unmeasurable and, to some extent, idiosyncratic. General patterns of repression may be discernible in different historical periods and I guess that the two major themes in relation to repressed affects (emotions) mentioned by Freud—sex and aggression—are still pertinent. Repression's dynamism and relation to the external world derives from the interaction between the parent, who is perceived as punitive, and the child. Here lies the basis of difference, incongruence and change. Parental modes of social control have changed, and are changeable at least over generations. The second possibility of change derives from the idiosyncratic nature of each child. Power differentials between parents and children underpin all repressive processes. With 'primal' repression, the content was never experienced consciously. However, with repression proper, the material was once conscious, but was experienced as being too threatening to the person's wellbeing and thus removed from consciousness. This is the repression Freud focused on. Many unconscious defence mechanisms are associated with repression and their basic function is to relieve the ego of intolerable anxiety.

I have chosen to follow Nancy Chodorow's explication of the relations between intra-psychic processes, family relationships and gender relations in our society. Chodorow's starting point is the observation that 'a crucial differentiating experience in male and female development arises out of the fact that women, universally, are largely responsible for early child care and for (at least) later female socialization'.[4] Her project is to account for the production and reproduction of the female personality in the first instance and, given the above premise, much of her focus is on parenting relations. Hence her object-relations approach. In contrast to such luminaries as Erikson, Freud, Horkheimer, Parsons and Spitz, who focus on the parent–son (in fact often the mother–son relations), Chodorow is particularly concerned with the (explicit) mother–daughter relations. Even though that is her aim, she frequently analyses the mother–son relations as well.

According to the object-relations school of psychoanalytic theory (for example, Balint, Fairbairn, Guntrip, Loewald, Winnicott) 'personality is a result of a boy's or girl's social-relational experience from earliest infancy. Personality development is not [merely] the result of conscious parental intentions'.[5] Thus, from the outset, the theorists whom Chodorow studies consider personality to arise from unconscious and conscious inter-personal relations, in contrast to Freud's individualistic internal approach underpinned by biological 'drives'. Aspects of personality such as self-concept and gender identity rest on the foundations of unconscious organisation. This is not to belie cultural expectations but to emphasise that both contribute to the production of personality.

Arising from the fact that women are generally the primary child carers in our society, the child's earliest experience is usually of identification with and attachment to one mother. Thus separation and individuation become powerful issues at various stages in the development of an individual adult. In this (pre-oedipal) primary identification with the mother, the child experiences the self as contiguous with the mother. This is a symbiotic relationship with biological underpinnings in that the foetus is part of the mother and the mother lactates, thus providing a life-support which involves a physical continuity between the mother and the suckling infant. This lack of differentiation, although physical in the first instance, becomes an emotional attachment of the baby to the mother and a reciprocal emotional bonding of the mother to the baby in our society.[6]

The traditional psychoanalytic model considers that the pre-oedipal experiences are similar for girls and boys. Following Klein and Deutsch, Chodorow points out that in mothering a daughter a woman experiences a double identification with both her own mother and her own daughter. Whether the identification by the mother with her mother is experienced if the child is a boy is not discussed. However I see no reason why it is not possible with a baby boy. The second aspect of the mother's double identification cannot appertain to a boy. What this signifies to Chodorow is that '[i]t seems likely that from their children's earliest childhood, mothers and women tend to identify more with daughters and to help them to differentiate less, and that processes of separation and individuation are made more difficult for girls'.[7] Thus pre-oedipal experiences of girls and boys are different in important aspects which impinge on the issues of separation and individuation. These experiences of separation versus symbiosis are revivified in adulthood as issues of independence versus dependence, which are significant problematic areas for violent males.

The oedipal crisis and resolution from which gender identity emerges is considered to begin after three years of age, although some theorists consider the establishment of 'core gender' a much earlier process.[8] The girl's oedipal task is to become sexually oriented to the male. 'In the traditional paradigm, a girl must change her love object from mother to father, her libidinal mode from active to passive, and finally her libidinal organ and eroticism from clitoris to vagina'.[9] Psychoanalytic theory at one level is a description of these processes. Classically a girl rejects her mother when she realises that her mother cannot give her the penis she lacks. Since Freud's 'penis envy' concept raises female hackles and is central to his theory of female development, we can at least consider it in a metaphorical light. Chodorow notes that Thompson (1943) (after Adler, 1927) suggests that penis envy 'is a symbolic expression of women's culturally devalued and underprivileged position in our patriarchal society' and the penis is therefore a symbol of 'power and privilege'.[10]

Chodorow objects to the vehemence with which some psychoanalysts claim the daughter rejects the mother. She sees the oedipal dilemma acted out against the background of Freud's description of the girl being 'attached' to her mother, rather than cathected to her, during the pre-oedipal phase. Thus 'a girl does not give up this pre-oedipal relationship completely, but rather builds whatever happens later upon this pre-oedipal base'.[11] Innate heterosexuality is the assumed drive behind the girl's envy of the penis and the desire of one for herself. Given Freud's claim for a 'polymorphous perverse' infant, heterosexuality cannot be assumed.[12] Chodorow considers conscious reasons for turning to the father which complement the unconscious turning towards him for the 'penis'. One is that the positive qualities of the mother—daughter relations may motivate her to look for other significant relationships. The other is that the father himself may encourage her to look towards him and she cites a range of empirical evidence to support this.[13] Thus the turning from the mother is due to both her positive attachment to her mother and her rejection of her mother because her mother is not the ultimate family powerbroker. The daughter's turning to her father is complemented by his turning to her with stereotyped gender expectations about how she should behave towards him as a heterosexual female child. Thus when the oedipal conflicts are resolved, the girl still identifies with her mother.

Freud's phallocentric theory (with himself inevitably at the centre) is permeated by mother focus and father non-focus. Whether this is due to the patriarchal practices and ideologies of middle-class (Jewish) Vienna or his own family experiences, or both, will never be totally clear. Marianne Krull[14] takes this further and considers that Freud's creative crises and theoretical deviations from previous directions are due to the power his father held over him at the conscious and unconscious levels. Taboos in relation to the father may well be intrinsic to his schema.

Women need to be vigilant with regard to such fears regarding the father and consequent theoretical privilege which accrues to the father. One attribute Freud has always given to the father is the superiority of the 'penis', actual and metaphorical. The metaphor is of power-wielding. A second privilege awarded to the father is lack of theoretical and empirical scrutiny. An untouchable, invisible inviolable father. The practical problems which arise from this are that what fathers are doing and not doing within the oedipal triangle have not been vigorously investigated at all in the last 90 years. As one half of the parenting pair is exempted from study, so the other half has been studied extensively. These studies are often by men, naturally with the patriarchal biases of psychoanalytic theory built in, and are not scrutinised or reflected upon. I could even go so far as to ask the question: was Freud needing to punish his mother as well as privilege his father?

Chodorow, with her focus on the daughter makes four points which I wish to apply to sons:

- the positive relationship with the mother in babyhood may be a social paradigm for sons, too, and reinforce them to seek such satisfying interactions with other people in his environment;
- the father himself will surely encourage his son to look to him;
- as the son is also born into a family with gendered power differences, he too should be attracted to the advantages of such patriarchal power and the person who embodies such advantages;
- the son's turning to his father is surely complemented by the father's articulated or inferred expectations of 'sonly' (male) qualities and behaviours.

The boy's oedipal task is to become sexually oriented to the female, which he has been in the pre-oedipal phase. Thus for the boy the gender of the love object remains the same, which implies that the achievement of heterosexuality is less complex than for the girl. The conflict for the boy devolves on the fact that his love object is his father's wife—thus he is ultimately in conflict with his father. So the boy's oedipal tasks are to repress the conflict with his father over his mother, retain the heterosexual love object orientation (but not for his mother) and identify with his father. No mean feat.

MALE POSITIONAL IDENTIFICATION

The most significant process I elaborate on in this chapter is that of positional male gender identification which derives from a father distancing himself (emotionally and physically) from active parenting. I present the process as an 'ideal' type. I present positional identification and its ramifications as a common male paradigm. No boy's gender identification will be totally 'positional', neither will any boy's gender identification be totally 'personal'. The two ideal types fall at either end of a continuum. Positional male gender identification allows for the incorporation of accessible cultural stereotypes of masculinity into the actual gender identity of the the male. This process incorporates macro-social behaviours into the intra-psychic processes; and it renders consciously apprehended material part of some unconscious processes. Thus the gendered male is reproduced in a particularly stereotyped way.

Positional identification involves identification with aspects of another person's role rather than with their personality, and does not necessarily lead to the internalisation of their values and attitudes. Thus identification processes have ramifications for superego development, as well as ego development, in that the internalisation of parental values is more coherent when nurturance and discipline emanate from the same source.[15]

It is within the family in the first instance that the meaning of masculinity is perceived by boys. The family is also the location in which expressions and behaviors associated with intimacy are experienced, observed and learned first of all. It is in this domain that methods of dealing with conflict are seen and absorbed.

The social context of positional identification[16] is that of patriarchal power relations and gendered divisions of labour in the public and private domains. Within this milieu, men have more power in relation to women than vice versa. And the division of labour within the family means that women will carry out most of the practical and emotional parenting activities. The under-involved and underresponsible father is the antecedent of the over-involved and over-responsible mother.

The employment responsibilities of most fathers in combination with the empirically verified emotional defensiveness of men[17] results in the distant father syndrome. The father is physically *and* emotionally distant from all family members in comparison to the mother. This is not an absolute status, but fathers may be conceptualised as falling along an affective and physically distant continuum. The affective is most significant and the two are not totally independent. This circumstance of father distance is crucial to the inner life of sons.

In our society at this stage of our history, the human infant needs positive and unconditional nurturance from its primary care givers. The infant of our species is emotionally dependent on its parents. Affective nurturance does not mean that if one parent offers a 'finite amount' of love, the other parent is affectively inconsequential.[18] As Seymour Epstein (along with object relations theorists and others such as Harry Stack Sullivan) points out, the emotional feedback received by the infant/young child from primary care givers determines how she/he feels about herself/himself. Thus a father's distance is at least as significant for the child's self-esteem as is the mother's closeness. The latter cannot 'make up for' the former in some quantitative way. It is the quality of the emotional responses from all primary care givers which makes up the infrastructure of the ego and the consequent sense of self-esteem.

The unconditional positive love of the father for the son will be very important for the boy during the pre-oedipal and oedipal period—or whenever his sense of being male is important to him. Thus the boy's ego and self-esteem is more dependent on positive emotional feedback from his father. If the boy feels secure in the positive affective messages he receives from males in his early life, he will develop 'personal identification' processes in which being male means being like his father figures.[19] These are the emotional circumstances in which most girls, raised by women, find themselves.

When the circumstances within the family do not satisfy the conditions necessary for 'personal identification', the child is 'forced' into 'positional identification' processes. The theorists from which Chodorow draws deem the latter identification processes to be less satisfying for the child. Positional identification forces the child to look to the world beyond his primary care givers for information about masculinity. This is how positional identification provides a bridge from the macro-social to the individual. The boy's circumstances allow him insufficient emotional access to masculinity within the family, so he seeks signs of maleness in the outside world. Television, of course, is his first resource. He will glean his nascent notions of masculinity from what he sees as male on television as well as other external sources.

Identification has unconscious and conscious elements and is basic to the construction of the ego. Thus positional identification bridges the levels of consciousness and the unconscious. Male stereotypes—signs of masculinity—as perceived and understood by the young boy become part of his unconscious make-up, part of his self and part of his self-evaluation and self-perception. Hence emotionally needy boys are doubly disadvantaged in that they are forced to seek signposts of maleness outside their primary care givers and the evidence that they see and hear even on children's television programmes is beyond their capacity to achieve succesfully.

Whilst in the oedipal phase, the possibility of fantasy is still open to these boys. Hence they see themselves driving cars, killing people, being strong, propelling rockets etc. Thus the male fantasies of one generation (television film-makers) feed into the male psyche of the next generation. When the 'magical' stage has passed, such boys are left aspiring towards cardboard cut-out portrayals of the male, feel already that they are 'failing' as males and develop compensatory mechanisms for this premature disappointment. Thus it is not hard to see that positionally identified males are going to lose more of themselves as each generation goes by and develop more extreme compensatory mechanisms—such as resorting to violence. Violence does not begin and end with violence towards intimates. Suicide, reckless driving and substance abuse are violence-against-self possibilities; as well as other outward oriented violence against property and persons known and unknown.

The most significant male positional identification process for the possibility of male violence is that the developing boy incorporates extant male stereotypical characteristics into his personality. These characteristics include toughness, strength and aggressiveness. The two basic factors which force boys into this kind of gender identification processes are the physical and the emotional distance of the fathers in the pre-oedipal (and later) stages of his growth. Father absence is filled by mother presence—but the former is the more pertinant problem for the boy. Talcott Parsons postulated as early as 1947 that these 'structural features of contemporary societies create a problem of masculine identification'.[20] Mothers, however, are popularly deemed to be the 'cause' of problems for men and boys. Mothers are more relevant to girls' gender identification processes which are commonly personal and comparatively less complicated. Fathers are the representatives of 'masculinity' within the family and it is towards his father that the boy looks to learn what it is to be a man.

If it is unclear what masculinity is, due to the inaccessibility of the father or the inchoate 'male' qualities of the father, signs of maleness will be sought elsewhere. I have not located any male authors who explicitly state that a father's physical presence within the home can still lead to a lack of clarity (from a young boy's perspective) about the essence of manhood.[21] In the previous chapter I noted that female activities and roles within the family and home are comparatively clear. The woman cares for children and husband emotionally and physically, she cooks and cleans and converses. If these are female domains, what else is there to do in a home? Should a boy conclude that a man cannot care, cannot cook, cannot clean and cannot converse? Or if the father does those things, is he less competent?

English and King reveal that fathers *do* discipline their children —that's a start. Stereotypical notions inform me that fathers may empty the garbage, mow the lawns and change the fuses. What do men do inside the home? They may watch television, drink beer, complain or brag about work, eat meals, play with their children and talk with their wife. What does differentiate fathers from mothers especially—since mothers may perform those activities too? My emphasis on doing is not simplistic— until the age of 12 years or so, children's cognitive abilities are such that they need clear and tangible evidence to allow them to make sense of masculinity. 'The cognitive limitations of pre-operational thought lead them [children] to rely on the visibility of concrete cues to define their gender and to ensure its permanence'.[22]

Male characteristics that are most readily discernible to a young boy are physical characteristics. Men are taller than boys, stronger, shaped in a more linear fashion, have deeper voices, grow facial hair and have a penis. Boys have none of these except a penis. Dorothy Ullian observes that:

> The discrepancy between the traits used by the young boy to define adult masculinity and his own existing attributes forces him to strive more intensely to ensure his male identity...In none of the attributes important to him, except the possession of a penis (which perhaps explains the young boy's preoccupation with it and its subsequent importance in theories of psychosocial development), is he like the man he wants, and is expected, to become.[23]

As these physical traits helped define masculinity, boys are likely to be concerned with being big, strong and having a penis. As adults, some men still seem to be concerned with those character-istics. I must note that one can display bigness and 'strength' by being violent.

Activities which may distinguish the father from the mother often take place outside the home. These are full-time work, watching or playing sport and drinking alcohol at the pub. Most-ly the boy is unable to observe his father at work or at the pub. He may watch sport (particularly 'male' games) with his father at home on television or at the sportsground. Overall, though, the young boy is hard pressed to delineate specific male attributes and activities that he can develop himself. Having a penis, watching (playing) sport and wielding power within the family are the most recognisable activities or qualities accessible to the child which enable him to comprehend the constituents of masculinity. If this is the case, it is not surprising to find sex, male sport and the defence of male authority significant in the lives of many men. The latter is particularly relevant to violent males in that some men may become violent to defend and reassert their perceived 'legitimate' authority within the family.

The main point of the previous discussion is that gender identity for males is comparatively difficult to achieve[24] within the modern family. This is even more important if the following contention by Ethel Person is true.

> Insofar as sexuality is a major component in the maintenance of gender, it is *crucial to identity*. There is a wealth of clinical evidence to suggest that, in this culture, genital sexual activity is a prominent feature in the maintenance of masculine gender while it is a variable feature in feminine gender.[25] [My emphasis]

Thus sexuality and gender are central to a person's sense of self, with sexuality being more important to the male identity. We can see from this that the positionally identified male is potentially in dire straits, in that masculinity is hard to grasp under capitalist-patriarchal child raising conditions but it is essential to the male's experience of his identity integrity. In his search for masculinity indicators, the young boy will need to look to more available sources than his father. Television of course is an excellent medium from which a boy may glean such information. Del Martin sardonically notes that:

> A boy who truly identifies with the role models reinforced by this society—for instance the brutal cops or paternalistic, know-it-all doctors and lawyers on television—would grow up with a version of . . . 'compulsive masculinity'.[26]

Compulsive masculinity is Talcott Parson's phrase to describe exaggerated stereotypical male behaviour, particularly roughness and toughness. It is these visible and concrete portrayals of masculinity that fill in the gaps for young boys. Two aspects of these stereotypes which are particularly relevant to violence being seen as a recognisable male quality are stereotypical prescriptions *for* male violence and *against* other forms of male expressions.[27] About one-third of Feldman's male adjectives are clearly conducive to violence, and nearly half proscribe expression of feelings. What is left? The remainder relate very much to the workplace— ambitious, competitive, enterprising, worldly, realistic—and one that is often forced into family relations—powerful.

These stereotypes are not somebody's idea of a bad joke but are derived from people's observations, writings and actual behavioural displays. Violence *is*, for some men, an actual as well as a stereotypical component of masculinity. Positional gender identification *is* a common enough circumstance in a boy's development in our society. Thus 'a particular segment of young boys may find the customary or acceptable range of masculine outlets too restrictive or too vague to guarantee the establishment of an unambiguous sexual identity'.[28] The media (and other macro-social sources) convey masculine images that are accessible, heroic, clever, violent, competitive, successful and unemotional. These characteristics of masculinity (adult men's wishful thinking and fantasies) are then integrated consciously and unconsciously into the young boy's gender identity, which is closely related to his sense of personal identity.

If 'masculinity' is difficult for the positionally identified boy to comprehend, 'femininity' within the modern family structure is more discernible. Thus the young male can recognise femininity and apply the principle that *masculinity is what femininity is not.*

As early as ages four and five, boys learn what is expected of them as males and restrict themselves to what they believe are suitably masculine activities. What this means in large part is not being like a girl, or what is the same thing, not being a 'sissy'.[29]

If masculinity is such a slippery status for males to grasp, the dichotomised sex stereotypes (determined, of course, by men) themselves may serve this very purpose of clearly delineating what is male and what is female. This need for males to know that they are masculine may also explain division of tasks by gender in so many families as exemplified by English and King's data. Thus it does not matter so much what the job is, but it does need to be clear within such families that this is the husband's arena and this is the wife's arena. The same circumstances frequently prevail in the workplace wherein specific tasks are deemed 'men's work' and others 'women's work'. In other words, it is not important whether the work relates to known expertise, but it is important that men always do activity X.

I believe that men who are violent towards women are particularly unsure of their masculinity.[30] In an effort to establish their maleness in their own eyes, they particularly adhere to dichotomised gender activities wihin the family. At a guess, this would mean doing minimal work within the house (perhaps staying out of it as much as possible) and doing minimal work with the children. On what the violent man might see as the 'positive' side, this would mean wearing an authoritative air around the house, drinking beer, watching 'male' sport and 'male' movies on television and possibly meting out excessive discipline to the children and making excessive demands of his wife. This description fits many male batterers as their subscription to rigid sex role stereotypes is well documented.

What being 'not like a girl' means to young boys grappling with the vagaries of masculinity is well expressed by Ruth Hartley.

> Boys believe grown-ups expect them to be noisy; to get dirty; to mess up the house; to be naughty; to be 'outside' more than girls are; not to be cry-babies; not to be 'softies'. . . Moreover, boys are not allowed to do the kind of things that girls usually do, but girls may do the kind of things that boys do.[31]

Clearly this is more helpful than no information on masculinity, but of course it is impossible given the codicil. If the boy has an older sister, she may well do 'everything' and do it well, and so what is left for her brother then? Being noisy, dirty and naughty, and of course not crying.

COGNITIVE–AFFECTIVE SPLIT AND NARROW EGO BOUNDARIES

Positionally identified boys learn to be male in a more conscious and less affective mode.[32] And male behaviours are less informed by feelings and conscience. The processes of male positional gender identification involves a schism between the father and discernible masculinity, between affection and gender role learning and between self and masculinity.[33] Chodorow compares female and male identification:

> Girls in contemporary society develop a personal identification with their mother, and. . .a tie between affective processes and role learning—between libidinal and ego development—characterizes feminine development. By contrast, boys develop a positional identification with aspects of the masculine role. For them, the tie between affective processes and role learning is broken.[34]

This cognitive–affective split has serious consequences for men in general as well as violent men in particular.

Broverman includes 'easily able to separate feelings from ideas' in her list of male behavioural characteristics, but in general it is not a male quality that is much discussed.[35] The significance of this split is that emotions are not incorporated into male decision-making.[36] Irrational behaviour (battering, rape, incest) is denied as such and 'explained' intellectually. Rationality does not inform male emotional life. Rationality without regard to quality of life, logical policies without regard to their personal ramifications and technical expertise without ethical considerations, are all general examples of the outcome of cognitive-affective dissociation at work in the public domain.

As positional identification takes place at a more conscious level than personal identification, there is another implied schism—of self and masculinity. One is 'in here', the other is consciously 'out there' and not necessarily part of one's self. This division allows for the possibility of disturbing doubts about whether one's self is male, or whether one is male enough. Thomas Ryan provides evidence for this conclusion.

> From the increased studies of sexuality and gender identity over the past two decades, it has become apparent that many more men than women experience problems about their gender identity. As a psychotherapist, I have increasingly observed from my clinical practice that men, in varying degrees, are either confused or in conflict about their sense of masculinity.[37]

Male violence against a female can be seen to be a desperate attempt by the perpetrator to prove to himself that he is *male*. Wife battering, rape and sexual assault of female children may serve this purpose well. As well as proving to himself that he is male, a violent man may also believe that he has proven his masculinity to his female victim as well. Another pragmatic aspect of choosing a woman as a target for violence is the 'sure winner' principle: 'Some men low in the status hierarchy seem to only exercise violence when they are assured of a victory'.[38] It is clear that the man who is violent towards a woman is protecting his gender too much.

Along with the emotional distance of fathers from sons inherent in male positional gender identification, the mother's identification with the male child is less intense. As discussed earlier, in parenting a female child, a mother identifies with her mother (as a mother) and identifies with the child as a daughter. With a male child, a mother identifies with her mother (as a mother) but she does not identify with the child as a son. Thus sons are not as emotionally bound to either parent.

The mother's double identification with her daughter allows female ego-boundaries to be wider and flexible. The differences between 'me' and 'you' in daughter–mother relationships in the early years of child development are traditionally not experienced as very rigid or clear. However the differences between 'me' and 'you' in son–mother relationships are usually experienced as being clearer. The mother relates to the son in boundary-creating ways and she is more likely to emphasise differences between herself and her son than she would between herself and her daughter. Thus male ego boundaries tend to be narrower and comparatively rigid.

The ramifications of these processes that have a bearing on male violence are threefold. One consequence of the differentiation between mother and son, in combination with the lack of affective closeness between father and son, is that sons may be forced to embark prematurely on a path of 'independence'. This is particularly fateful in that the male gender stereotype emphasises independence. What happens to a child who is not allowed (consciously or unconsciously) to experience the level of emotional dependence he needs for his personal security? I contend that such a child as an adult will *fear emotional dependence*. In adulthood, the experience of intimacy will result in an ambivalent response towards the person with whom he is intimate. This ambivalence derives from the powerful unsatisfied (or unresolved) need for emotional dependence and the internal and external proscription against male emotional dependence. Much of the literature describing male batterers acknowledges that such men have 'unresolved dependency needs'.

The second characteristic arising from male narrow ego boundaries is a narrow sense of responsibility for self. If there is a small emotional and practical 'space' around me which is mine then that is all I can be responsible for. Thus I cannot be blamed for experiences and activities that seem to be out there away from me. This is a paradigm for projection. Projection is an

> unconscious mechanism in which a person attributes to another those generally unconscious ideas, thoughts, feelings, and impulses that are in himself undesirable or unacceptable. Projection protects the person from anxiety arising from an inner conflict.[39]

Violent males are frequently described as over-utilisers of the defence mechanism projection. The essence of projection is that acts I have perpetrated are experienced as not being my responsibility—they are the fault of others. Thus the male batterer blames his wife for his violence towards her. Frequently male batterers make such statements and the rationalisations to an outsider read as quite bizarre. However such persons who unconsciously resort to the overuse of the defence mechanism of projection actually believe that their actions are the other person's fault. (Projection is not the exclusive domain of males but I believe that the nature of male ego boundaries increases the likelihood that males will project blame at a greater rate than females). Society colludes at times with such male projections: her nagging causes his battering; her physique causes his rape; and a child's innocence is interpreted as being seductive towards a grown man.

The third consequence of narrow ego boundaries, and related to superego development, is that the propensity for experiencing guilt is diminished. Males are less prone to the experience of appropriate guilt. Here I take a position exactly in opposition to Freud, and offer three explanations for my audacity. Firstly, the argument described above is logical. Secondly, I see practical evidence of this in the public domain, the private domain and recognise it in clinical case histories. Thirdly, I believe that Freud was blinded by his own position within the patriarchal structures.[40] The 'natural' analogies he would make would be those of 'masculinity' and 'civilisation', civilisation and a highly developed superego. Along with blaming others for their actions, males are less likely to feel shame or guilt about those particular actions. Again, this is related to narrow and rigid ego boundaries within which the male feels and acts. Descriptions of male batterers sometimes mention that the first act of violence towards a given female partner is followed by guilt, shame, remorse and attempts to make up. This cycle of violence, followed by guilt and repentance, may last for years in some men but it rarely lasts for longer than five years. Thus, in male batterers, it seems that 'normal' and appropriate guilt in response to extreme violence towards a 'loved one' may be experienced, but it is underdeveloped.

Having explained in detail the consequences of positional identification for the male, such outcomes can be contrasted with a picture of an hypothesised, personally identified male. This male will identify directly with his father as a person. His father will convey overt as well as unconscious messages (these are likely to be both positive and negative to some extent) about being male which the son will introject. This will create feelings of security about self and gender and male stereotypes will not necessarily impinge on the son's psyche in a very personally meaningful way. He will have feelings of attachment to both his father and mother and these feelings will inform his thinking and his sexuality. Thus, ethics and morality will be part of his daily living and inform intellectual, technical and rational activities. Such a male will be truly independent and take responsibility for himself and his actions, that is, his conscience will be appropriate to his behaviours. He will not be emotionally dependent to the extent that his relations with women will have a hidden agenda in relation to these needs. This authentic independence allows for interdependent relationships with mutual respect.

As a result of the father's distance, girls remain emotionally attached to their mothers. Thus the female resolution of the oedipus complex is an *erotic* orientation towards the father and males and, because of their strong attachment to their mothers, men remain *emotionally* secondary.[41] The male resolution is an erotic *and* an emotional orientation towards the mother and females.[42] The male is therefore in the potentially anxious position of having all of his erotic and emotional (conscious and unconscious) eggs in one basket. Any resentments he bears in relation to his mother (and we all carry some) may be acted out towards his female intimate. Anger from the past—barely recognised by the actor—may become violence today.

These processes relate to male violence towards intimates in that intimacy (or at least proximity in the spousal relationship) may resonate unconsciously with the paradigmatic emotional attachment in the man's life, that is, with his mother. Thus 'unfinished business' devolving on the omnipotent mother may resurface with any affective (particularly heterosexual) closeness. This emotional proximity is even more disturbing in that it falls outside the defining characteristics of the male positional role itself. (It is important to emphasise as Nancy Chodorow does that 'paradigmatic attachment' and 'omnipotent mother' are not mother-blaming terms here as they have been in the psychoanalytic and psychiatric literature, but are social-capitalist-patriarchal constructions. The mother–infant relationship is only paradigmatic in that there is no father–infant relationship to equal its intensity. The mother is only omnipotent and omnipresent because the father is neither).

Male positional identification is significant for male violence in general in that violence is a socially acceptable aspect of the male role in some social groups. Furthermore, males may commit violence against others without feeling guilty themselves or deemed guilty in the legal sense by others. If there is an inchoate experience of remorse, the dissociated cognitive facilities can conjure up 'reasons' for the criminal act—the rationalisations that abound in wife batterers' presentations of their stories. Positional identification has particular significance in relation to violence towards women in that women are the 'other'—everything that is not male. This provides fertile ground for the unconscious mechanism of projection that also characterises wife batterers.

I suggest that either having sex, or affective ties, with a woman may be unsettling for a man whose gender identificational processes during his development were positional. Hence the possibility of sex and violence (including murder in the extreme) and violence against a female intimate (including murder in the extreme). The violence of course is not inherent in the fears arising unconsciously from sex and/or intimacy, but violence is implicit in the stereotypical repertoire available to males to enable them to 'cope' with difficulties. And wife batterers are often described as being fearful of intimacy.[43] There is less evidence that sex is problematic, but at least one researcher found that wife batterers frequently doubted their virility, were impotent and made excessive sexual demands.[44]

OTHER EVIDENCE

Andrew Tolson is one of the few male sociologists to broach these issues. He does not use a psychoanalytic framework but rather more his own observations and descriptive skills. His approach to the male experience of masculinity fits in with the conclusions Nancy Chodorow has drawn. Tolson focuses on the absence of the father from the family, and the comparative emotional distance of fathers from sons. He describes the 'ambivalence' of the son in relation to masculinity. '. . .masculinity is both mysterious and attractive (in its promise of a world of work and power) and yet, at the same time, threatening (in its strangeness, and emotional distance)'.[45] He is acknowledging the contradictions inherent in masculinity, particularly in working class masculinity. Power is promised, but is it forthcoming?

The boy's apprehension of the promise and threat of masculinity is an analog of his awareness of his father's power within the family and his emotional distance from his son. This situation aptly describes the sundered relations between affect and identification in the male child. Tolson takes this further.

> A boy's identification with his father is the *foundation* for *all* his subsequent experience. . .In the culture of masculinity, rewards are always distant, at a premium. They must be fought over, competitively, through a long struggle for supremacy.[46] [My emphases]

Here Tolson highlights the father in an extreme fashion: he is claiming that the father–son relations are a matrix for all future relational experience. His language use is significant. 'Fighting', 'competing' and 'struggling' are related to masculinity and social rewards. Furthermore, Tolson considers the boy's appreciation of the contradictions of masculinity with its connotations of future power, and the inaccessibility of power sets him up to 'struggle' for what has been promised, albeit vaguely by the father. This struggle begins with father, and the development of the practices and notions of 'masculinity' evolve during the boy's early years within the family, at school and amongst peers.

Tolson acknowledges different class 'styles' of masculinity but emphasises a commonality.

> What working- and middle-class boys have in common is the masculine emotional structure—the basis of all subsequent personality development, whether it is in terms of self-motivated ambition, or aggressive authoritarianism, the masculine personality is commonly built upon an ambivalent relationship with one's father.[47]

He sees the distance of the father, how the mother accounts for the father and the contradictory representations of masculinity as crossing class lines and he therefore emphasises the similarities between male experiences rather than the differences. These cross-class similarities are nascently violent whether it is the middle class striving for success or working class physical aggression.

Tolson considers the main male activities at school to be sporting and intellectual competitiveness, the discovery of sexuality and the experience of complex male hierarchies. As fathers do not often discuss sex or relationships with their sons, boys learn about sex from their school friends.

> This means that sex is, from the first, part of the competitive boyhood culture, in which the insecure individual seeks confirmation in ritual jokes and camaraderie. Sexual experience becomes part of the hierarchy.[48]

The boy's information about work is second-hand in the first instance as is information about sex. Whereas school prevents 'working' to a large extent, the male subculture encourages first-hand experience with females in some guise or other. 'And the group's communication is a self-sustaining network of boasting, half-truth, and fabrication, in which it is impossible to distinguish reality from fiction'.[49] Here Tolson clearly associates sex with male competition and male group coherence.

Since Tolson claims masculinity itself is confused and intertwined with fantasy, it may not be surprising that sexual relations with females are also fertile gounds for an entanglement of fantasies of seduction and being seduced and the ghastly reality of making apparently purposeful moves into unknown territory. Tolson believes that

> a masculine education drives a wedge between external behaviour and inner experience: the development of the former blocks the expression of the latter. There is, in the end, no recognized channel by which a boy can either communicate his feelings to others, or discover their possibilities within himself.[50]

This may be an echo of processes I have discussed earlier. The boy whose identification with his father is positional does not have strong positive affective bonds with his father. Inner experiences *are* affective. The external behaviour pertaining to the expression of masculinity is, by virtue of the processes of positional identification, bereft of affect. Without the emotional concomitants of learning, masculine behaviour has no connection to inner experience. The primary identification of the boy with his mother is a strong inner experience, but it is one that he must deny if his mode of identifying with his father is positional. This situation is pregnant with conscious and unconscious repercussions when the adult male forms intimate relationships with adult females.

Tolson's book, *The Limits of Masculinity*, emphasizes the roles of fathers of boys in the trajectory of the boy to manhood. He acknowledges the distance of fathers from sons and of masculinity from boys. His work is important, not for its academic rigour, but because he is brave enough as a male in our patriarchal society to face the father in the family. This is a difficulty which is displayed in a plethora of ways by male psychiatrists, sociologists and psychologists, even when the evidence is on the page that the fathers' contributions should be seriously studied.[51]

4 | Male violence, female target: the low self-esteem and high emotional dependency nexus

> All my life I have been haunted by the obsession that to desire a thing or to love a thing intensely is to place yourself in a vulnerable position, to be a possible, if not a probable, loser of what you most want.
>
> 1959 foreword to *Sweet Bird of Youth* Tennessee Williams

In chapters 1 and 2 I discussed major social structures which derive from patriarchy and capitalism and impinge on all men and women in our society. Then in chapter 3 I looked at male gender construction along a father-distance continuum within the context of gendered power structures. In this chapter I focus on low male self-esteem and high emotional dependency which derive from the above factors and manifest themselves along two continua in our male population. Patriarchy, the family and male gender construction are necessary factors which contribute to male violence and affect *all* men in our society. *Low* self-esteem and *high* emotional dependency, in combination with the structural factors from which they emerge, are *sufficient* for a male in our society to be violent. A significant issue is that low self-esteem and high emotional dependency are likely to be established by the present 'normal' processes involved in male gender construction and reproduction.

THE GENESIS OF LOW SELF-ESTEEM

Lenore Walker, one of the leading researchers of battered women, produces the following description of batterers:

75

- has low self-esteem;
- believes all the myths about battering relationships;
- is a traditionalist believing in male supremacy and the stereo-typed masculine sex role in the family;
- blames others for his actions;
- is pathologically jealous;
- presents a dual personality;
- has severe stress reactions, during which he uses drinking and wife battering to cope;
- frequently uses sex as an act of aggression to enhance self-esteem in view of waning virility—may be bisexual;
- does not believe his violent behaviour should have negative consequences.[1]

Mildred Pagelow interviewed Michael Wellins who had been counselling battering men for fifteen years, and he offered a similar account.

> The overall impression he has gained from the men are that they (1) have a deep sense of inadequacy, (2) had authoritarian homes, and (3) had poor role models. As a result, they feel ugly about themselves, lack self-esteem, and try aggressive ways to maintain whatever self-esteem they have left.[2]

At this juncture I need to define self-esteem, as it is a term used frequently, is rarely defined and many writers use it in ways that are different to my own understanding of it. Seymour Epstein provides an appropriate and comprehensive definition.

> ...self-esteem is one of the most basic postulates in an individual's implicit theory of reality. It is highly resistant to enduring change and, when it does change, it induces profound changes throughout the entire conceptual system. Self-esteem is equivalent to self-love or love worthiness. It is initially derived from the internalization of the love relationship with the parents. Just as the parents once automatically bestowed and withheld love according to their evaluation of the child's behaviour, the child learns to bestow love on itself and withhold love according to the child's evaluation of its own behaviour. By internalizing the parents' reaction, the child is provided with a highly effective tool for controlling its behaviour in a manner that makes the behaviour conform to the parents' values...Accordingly, self-evaluation is apt to be learned under conditions of intense emotional involvement, which are the conditions assumed to generate postulates that are highly general and resistant to modification.[3]

Epstein believes that self-esteem derives from the unconscious internalisation of the love relationships with the parents. If the mother behaves lovingly towards her son and the father does not, the basis for a positive sense of self is inherently shaky. Should the father interact with the male child from an emotional distance, the child may feel that he is not lovable enough for his father. This may be perceived by the child as paternal rejection, that is, he—the child—is not good enough for his father's love. These processes may be the first experience of a distance in his father which the son *feels* is to do with his *own* inferiority. Paul Amato drew the following conclusions after his recent Australian research:

> Many children in the study complained that their fathers were not interested in them and said that they wished for more time and help from their fathers. It was also shown. . . that lack of attention from fathers was related to low self-esteem, low self-control, low life skills, and low social competence among sons and daughters of primary school age. These findings indicate that the importance of the father-child bond should not be underestimated.[4]

The kernel of self-esteem develops early in life and is closely related to love and affection expressed by the parents to the child. Development of the 'self' is a series of processes beginning early in infancy. The self derives from internal and interactional physiological experiences with the mother in the first instance. The ego ensues. As the ego develops, so does self-perception and self-evaluation. Edith Jacobsen highlights the affective underpinnings of self-esteem.

> Whereas self perception always represents an ego function, the self evaluation of an adult person is not exclusively a superego function. Founded on subjective inner experience and on objective perception by the ego of the physical and mental self, it is partly or sometimes predominantly exercised by the superego, but is also partly a critical ego function whose maturation weakens the power of the superego over the ego. Self esteem is the ideational, especially the emotional, expression of self-evaluation.[5]

Thus self-esteem is particularly the affective aspects of self evaluation which arises from the developing ego as much as from the superego. As children develop beyond the pre-verbal stage, they form cognitive views that complement their learned feelings about themselves.[6] Hence, self-esteem is secured, to a large extent, very early in life, even though it continues to develop throughout the latency phase of childhood and is not considered to be finally consolidated until the issues of adolescence are resolved.

Erich Fromm's conception of adult self-love is similar to the concept of self-esteem I am using.

Not only others, but we ourselves are the 'object' of our feelings and attitudes; the attitudes towards others and towards ourselves far from being contradictory, are basically *conjunctive*...an attitude of love towards themselves will be found in all those who are capable of loving others...Genuine love is an expression of productiveness and implies care, respect, responsibility and knowledge.[7]

Adequate self-esteem can therefore be translated as self-love. The self-love of an individual is reflected in the ability to wholesomely love others. Thus self-esteem is a critical concept for comprehending the quality of 'love' relationships.

Many researchers in the field of wife battering see the primary characteristic of male batterers as that of low self-esteem.[8] According to Rollo May, 'deeds of violence in our society are performed largely by those trying to establish their self-esteem'.[9] Here low self-esteem and violence are postulated as two sides of one coin. The coin in our society is, of course, male.

Anthony Storr acknowledges the inverse relationship between the two in males.

The lower a person's sense of self-esteem, the more does he have recourse to paranoid mechanisms to sustain what little feeling of worth he possesses, and the more vulnerable he is to having that little undermined. It is the insecure and inadequate who most easily feel threatened, and who resort to violence as a primitive way of restoring dominance.[10]

Psychoanalysts like May and Storr recognise the apparently paradoxical connections between low self-esteem and violence. That self-esteem is a process beginning early in life, leads me to believe that low self-esteem and violence in males are connected in male positional gender identification.

As low self-esteem is a precursor of violence, I wish to attempt an answer to the question, Is being male predisposing to low self-esteem? Some readers may laugh and say, 'Males—they have public and private power, they earn more money, they devise policy and pass legislation. How could they be candidates for low self-esteem?' It may be that the disjuncture between what some males claim are male rights, and what the majority of males experience, sets up circumstances for feelings of 'failure'. In his study of success and sport Michael Messner concluded that even highly skilled athletes are highly likely to view themselves as failures.

The disjuncture between the *ideology* of success and the socially structured *reality* that most do not 'succeed' brings about widespread feelings of failure lowered self-images and problems with interpersonal relationships.[11]

How achievable are the 'ideals' embedded in male stereotypes? As well as Larry Feldman's compendium which I have elaborated on in chapter 2, Marc Fasteau lists over 40 male characteristics derived from studying 980 American adults with a range of educational levels, across the major religions, either married or single. Traits proferred by the respondents include: very aggressive; very independent; like math and science very much; very competitive; very logical; know the ways of the world; almost always act as a leader; very self-confident; very ambitious; not at all talkative.[12] What proportion of the male population actually has those characteristics? Del Martin produces a similar list of adjectives cited in various definitions of 'masculine'. Her list includes: brave; analytical; virile; intellectual; farsighted; profound; authoritarian; self-sufficient.[13] How achievable are those characteristics for most men?

Battering men have low self-esteem. All men with low self-esteem are not batterers but we cannot ignore this potential. From the male stereotypical prescriptions, it seems to me that if a male were to take them seriously he would have to acknowledge that he could not live up to (or down to) most of them. The search for gender identity does not begin in adulthood but all of the stereotypical 'ideals' apply to men rather than boys. What qualities do *boys* perceive as being male and are they achievable? 'The young boy not only fails to possess the required masculine attributes of the adult male, but he is often physically and intellectually inferior *even* to the female child on many of these dimensions'.[14]

Dorothy Ullian believes that a boy who is unsure about what being a boy means can, within the stereotypical range, resort to

an excessive amount of competition, aggression, and anger (behaviour often labelled 'acting-out' and inevitably interfering with school-related learning) (which) may represent a necessary, albeit exaggerated response to the developmental task of establishing a clear and stable male identity. One might speculate that the predominance of male children as candidates for behavioural and emotional problems, acting-out behaviour, and learning disorders may be at least partially explained by this formulation.[15]

Thus boyhood perceptions of masculinity may not be achievable for a range of boys for various reasons.

As well as an early specialisation in aggressive behaviour and competitions in strength, speed and endurance in the schoolyard, the boy with tenuous self-esteem and positional gender identification may be bothered by his own personal qualities that could be deemed 'female'.

> Young children of both sexes describe women as small, physically powerless, gentle and pretty, with high-pitched voices and soft skin...Unable to distinguish physical from psychological attributes, children at this age (4–7 years) conclude that women, by nature, are 'nicer' and 'softer', 'cry more easily', and are more capable of rearing children.[16]

Thus being nice, soft, crying or looking after younger children may be behaviours the young boy aims not to reveal in himself, if his self-esteem is marginal and masculinity is problematic.

To make matters worse for him, the young boy is comparatively small, weak and hairless on face and body and has a high-pitched voice. The boy has no control over these inevitable physical characteristics, thus being 'difficult', 'rough', not crying and ignoring younger children are qualities that are actually achievable. This scenario is not too different from that which Ruth Hartley discerned in boys.

> They believe grown-ups expect them to be noisy; to get dirty; to mess up the house; to be naughty; to be 'outside' more than girls are; not to be cry-babies; not to be 'softies', not to be 'behind' like girls are; and to get into trouble more than girls do.[17]

According to boys, this is what their parents expect of them. So the situation of the young boy is exacerbated by parental demands which include directives that are not productive (for example, being naughty) and others that are the opposite to what girls are allowed to do (for example, not crying). There is plenty of potential for boys to be wary of displaying a range of traits or behaviours which could be labelled 'sissy' by parents or by other children.[18] Thus positionally identified boys seeking signs of maleness are on a trajectory towards low self-esteem and unachievable 'masculine' traits.

The male becomes separated from himself by virtue of his affective experience being denied, denigrated or displaced. If a man experiences his feelings as alien and is taught not to trust them, then he cannot trust himself. If he cannot trust himself he cannot trust others—a highly anxiety-producing situation. Being separated from one's self and one's feelings is not conducive to a positive sense of self-esteem. And it is not conducive to empathy with another's pain, or remorse at one's violence.

SIGNIFIERS OF MASCULINITY: SPORT, WORK, ALCOHOL AND POWER OVER WOMEN

How are men meant to excel in the world? Sport, work, drinking alcohol, being 'head' of the household and being violent are possible arenas for these purposes. Marc Fasteau goes as far as claiming that being athletic is the *sine qua non* of masculinity. 'Pressure from parents, nearly always fathers, peers, and other male adults, results in a skewing of values which tend to make sports a compulsion for many boys, the mandated centre of their lives'.[19] In the domain of sports, boys can acceptably display their competitiveness and aggressiveness and persuade their fathers, their coaches and themselves that they are all indeed male.[20] Messner declares 'It is likely that the rise of football as "America's number-one game" is largely the result of the comforting *clarity* it provides between the polarities of traditional male power, strength, and violence.'[21]

Work is another 'productive' domain in which males can establish their identity and their self worth. Paul Willis observes that

> [work based] self-esteem derives from the achievement of a purpose which not all—particularly women—are held capable of achieving. The wage packet is the provider of freedom, and independence: the particular prize of masculinity in work.[22]

Since such importance is attributed by males to sport and work, this makes the patriarchal structures of sport and work in our society more comprehensible. If these domains allow men to compete, be aggressive and enhance their masculinity, sport for both sexes and jobs in which women could excel will be problematic. Presumably if women can play sport X or do occupation Y, men cannot gain kudos in masculinity from such activities. Hence, sports which are predominantly male are those that best satisfy the conditions, for example, football, cricket and wrestling. Gender segregation in the workplace helps some males feel that their work is men's work, therefore they are men. 'There is nothing inherent in jobs that makes them either appropriately female or male. If anything remains fixed, it is the *distinction* between men's work and women's work'.[23]

One cannot help but wonder what male needs inspire the vigour with which male space and place at work are fought for. According to a Leeds trade union study, twice the number (96 per cent) of women employed in journalism, police work and certain manual trades—so-called male jobs—experienced sexual harassment in comparison to women in 'non-male' areas.[24] The harassment is also twice as intensive, twice as persistent and twice as likely to be carried out by co-workers than by supervisory men. Thus in traditionally segregated areas, the men resist desegregation; but once women become co-workers, the men appear to work hard to keep the women in their 'sexual place'.

As well as keeping women out or down, these practices may

be men-oriented as well. Men who have no authentic sense of camaraderie in relation to each other may resort to practices and topics of conversation which they believe all men should be able to contribute to. Conversations which denigrate and sexually objectify women, along with endless discussions about sport and cars, may serve such purposes as they are indirect attempts to form some sort of male solidarity. Non-physical forms of sexual harassment—pin-ups, talking about sexual activities, 'wolf' whistling, etc.—may be as much for mutual male benefit as they are an embarrassment to many females.[25]

Sport is, by and large, geared to winning these days. This means that even sporting males may not become 'stars' or play for the winning side. And, of course, some men learned early that they failed at sport and withdrew. Work, perhaps to a lesser extent, is also geared to winning. A significant fact, though, is that all workers in the public domain receive pay. Some men do boring jobs, some men work with women and some men's wives work. Of course only a few men are at the top of the ladder, although it seems that lots of little ladders are erected so that more men can at least claim they are climbing one. The final problem with work as an endorser of masculinity is that a proportion of the male workforce is inevitably unemployed.

Even though the workplace can be expected to treat middle class and upper class men well, this is not necessarily the case. 'No matter how high a man goes in the economic, political or educational world, there are always other persons who either have more power or who are capable of stripping him of his power'.[26] On the other hand Mike Donaldson discerns that

> work made meaningless by capitalist social relations is given
> significance by patriarchy. The necessity to do boring, repetitive,
> dirty, unhealthy, demeaning, self-destructive, mind-numbing,
> soul-destroying work is turned into a virtue.[27]

Male workers (as well as female workers) can be quite resourceful and creative in getting something positive out of their hard or dreary work. Thus there are contradictions in the work experiences of men of all classes. Some working class men may gain a sense of personal achievement from their daily grind.[28] Some upper middle class men may find their work frustrating and soul destroying even though they have high occupational status, wield power and earn a substantial income.

Working class respondents are generally optimistic about moving up the work hierarchy, and just over half in one survey believed it was possible to reach the top by virtue of skill and hard work.[29] There may be, in the first instance, a general view of hopefulness about their own and their friends' chances in their working lives, although some work experiences may not justify this optimism. Claire Williams found that about three-quarters of the Queensland miners she studied considered that there was a serious discrepancy between the amount of work autonomy they were allowed and the amount they believed they should have.[30] Even though such anomalies are causes of grievances, they can also facilitate worker solidarity in attempts to squeeze improved working conditions from the bosses. 'There is some manliness in being able to stand up to the giant'.[31] Thus working class men derive some positive gains from their work, not necessarily intrinsic to it but related to their experience of male unity in their exploitation and in their endeavours to gain mutual and personal benefits from these circumstances.

Williams argues that 'male working-class chauvinism is a vital cultural defence for men against exploitation in their work environment, which is then carried back to the home'.[32] Thus, when working men do not experience work as sufficiently rewarding, they can attempt to compensate for being treated as inferiors in the workplace by behaving in what they consider to be a superior fashion in relation to members of their family. Furthermore, they can displace feelings of frustration experienced in the workplace onto spouse and/or children.

According to Mildred Pagelow, some men are violent towards their wives to compensate for

> powerlessness elsewhere, they are scapegoating...this occurs when goal-directed persons become angry and hostile when their desires are frustrated. They are stymied and they do not know who or what is blocking them from their goals. Sometimes they do know, but the obstacle is too powerful or fearsome to fight directly, so they find weaker targets who cannot retaliate.[33]

This line of argument is frequently purveyed by sociologists, particularly those who prefer to believe that male violence is confined to the working class and unemployed. However these circumstances pertain as much to middle class men, whose expectations of work rewards may be high but unfulfilled. Male violence occurs in all classes in our society.

If a male is low on self-esteem, unsure of his gender identity, has given up playing sport to watch it and he is unemployed, what avenues are left to him? Drinking alcohol is one. Women drink alcohol, but great numbers of women do not do so in public places to a great extent. Thus the public bar provides a mostly male venue for males who need to do something male with other men who are doing it too. Drinking compatriots will tell them that they are men directly and indirectly in return for their mates doing the same for them. There may even be some pubs which are more 'male' than others, some alcoholic drinks which are more 'male' than others, along with the belief that consuming a huge volume of alcohol is a 'male' talent.

> The connection between alcohol consumption and manliness may seem so obvious as to appear a truism. It is therefore surprising that no cohesive presentation has documented the ties between traditional sex roles and men's alcohol use.[34]

Russell Lemle and Marc Mishkind, who make this paradoxical statement, carried out a broad-ranging literature search in an attempt to discern the relationships between masculinity and alcohol consumption. Men drink 30 to 100 per cent more alcohol than women on a given occasion; men consume alcohol twice as often and become intoxicated twice as often; there are three to four times as many male 'heavy' drinkers, 'problem' drinkers and alcoholics as there are female. These differences are so common that they exist across all age groups, regions, religions, education and income levels and ethnic groups within industrialised western societies.[35]

Lemle and Mishkind consider how alcohol drinking symbolises masculinity in our society. They believe that this starts at an early age. Along with a male's first sexual experience, his first alcohol experience is likely to be a fundamental initiation process. Men drink alcohol in male company more often than women do in female company. To 'drink like a man' one must consume it 'straight'; not sweeten it; prefer beer and spirits; drink without hesitation; and 'hold his liquor' without becoming obviously drunk or addicted.[36]

The media has reflected and created close connections between alcohol consumption and maleness. Over half of 700 alcohol commercials (in 1982 in the United States) showed 'macho' males taking a break from 'male' activities for a drink (mostly beer). Beer advertisements portray beer as advancing men in male organisations and uniting men in brotherhood. The major American beer producer sponsors 92 per cent of major league baseball teams and 71 per cent of national league football teams in 1988. Advertisements for spirits are overrepresented in sexually oriented magazines targeting male readership. In *Playboy* alcohol accounts for 22 per cent of advertisements compared to 7 per cent in magazines in general.[37]

Alcohol consumption is linked to the 'male' characteristics of risk-taking and aggressiveness. Risk-taking is perhaps by definition a difficult activity. Males are expected to consume a lot of alcohol often; but they are not exemplifying manliness when they indulge in morose self-pity; nor is being an alcoholic a manly activity. Men who are 'normal' alcohol drinkers increase their levels of verbal and physical aggression in laboratory studies. Even men who had been led to believe that they had consumed alcohol behaved more aggressively even though they had not.[38] Such are the strongly held associations between aggression and alcohol. For some males it would be legitimate to blame alcohol for their violence, rather than take responsibility for themselves.

The option of drinking alcohol to enhance one's masculinity is available to any male who can afford some drinks. Many studies reveal an association between alcohol consumption rates in men and wife abuse.[39] Some have compared battering and non-battering couples (Vincent Van Hasselt *et al*), and others have gained the information from large nationally representative samples. Morton Bard and Joseph Zacker consider that battered women's information about their husband's alcohol use may be coloured by the lay view of alcohol being an acceptable 'cause' of violence. They also believe that the same sort of logic may apply to policemen. After special training, a group of (American) police officers determined that alcohol was the basic factor behind wife assault in only 14 per cent of 1388 family disputes.[40]

Nevertheless there is an association between the two. This does not mean that all or most alcoholics are wife abusers, neither does it mean that most wife abusers have an alcohol problem. It is possible that, where there is a relationship between alcohol abuse and wife battering, the two may have a similar etiology rather than a causal relationship. Some authors consider excessive rates of alcohol consumption amongst working class males are related to structural factors in the workplace. Others also consider that structural frustrations in the workplace contribute to wife battering. Both wife battering and alcohol use/abuse may be attempts by men with low self-esteem and gender insecurity to decrease both of these deficits by indulging in 'appropriate' activities available to them.[41] This could account for the higher rates of wife battering amongst the working classes. If their gender identification is positional, their self-esteem shaky, work or sport are closed to them or work is a frustration in itself, then drinking with the 'boys' may make them feel like 'men'. Behaving in an authoritarian way at home may also provide a similar opportunity. Thus alcohol use/abuse and violence towards wives may have similar roots and therefore present as a correlation in some studies.

As with the commonplace associations between masculinity and alcohol, there is an even more obvious connection between masculinity and sexual activity. Richard Dyer comments ironically that:

> One would think that writing about images of male sexuality would be as easy as anything...Male sexuality is a bit like air—you breathe it in all the time, but you aren't aware of it much.[42]

The above quotation appears in *The Sexuality of Men* which says surprisingly little about males and sex but reveals other related information. Such texts are beginning to mitigate against the views of men that men in power have presented to us all. Peter Filene notes that:

> The histories that men have written about themselves, then, contain the same bias as the histories they have written about one another. The three-dimensional man—private, semipublic, and public—is flattened into a masculine stereotype, an image who poses like the Marlboro man on a billboard beside the highway.[43]

According to Tony Eardley, the majority of men interviewed by Shere Hite for the *Hite Report*, listed sexual intercourse as the most important sexual activity; and they believed they didn't have sex often enough.

> There seems to be a tension within masculinity itself—a tension between the compulsive and regimenting demands of masculine socialization and the desire to express a variety of needs and emotions which...often have little intrinsically to do with sex at all.[44]

A number of authors acknowledge this social and personal conflation of sexual and other needs.[45] Vic Seidler articulates this most clearly and pungently.

> Our sexual needs are given more public recognition and seen to confirm our masculinity rather than threaten it. For this reason we go for sexual contact as a way of fulfilling our needs for dependency.[46]

Emotional dependency arises from positional identification when the father is rejecting or punitive towards his son. This lack of love creates an emotional neediness. The social script is such that it is forbidden for sons as adults to seek such nurturance from their (still) distant fathers, thus parenting is sought from more acceptable quarters—from women. Thus female spouses are overtly acknowledged as sex partners but used as ever-giving and over-tolerant mothers (parents).

Another possibility for the non-sporting man with a non-satisfying job is endeavouring to enhance his self-esteem and masculinity in comparison to, or in relation to, females. This would include sexual 'conquests' and having 'lots' of sex and/or 'lots' of lovers. A not necessarily sexual variation on the theme would include being the 'boss' at home. Such men may bully, humiliate, or make excessive demands of their wives. They may also be violent. Erich Fromm calls these men sadists.

> I see the passion to control another being, that is, to completely control, to have in my power, to do with [her] what I will, to be, so to speak, [her] god, to be almighty. This situation is realized in the form of injuring someone else, to humble [her] physically, so that [she] cannot defend [herself]. With sadism, it must be that the other person is helpless and weak. Sadism never has a strong person as an object...The more powerless a person is, the more likely he is to compensate for his weakness by sadism.[47]

Fromm's sadist is a man who has a poor view of himself and who feels more powerful when he injures and humbles his wife. She is not as physically strong as him (he is a 'sure winner') and patriarchal societal structures provide her with less access to protection, justice or retribution than *he* would have should someone outside his family assault *him*.

Thus a male with low self-esteem may take recourse to battering his wife, raping a woman or sexually assaulting his child to make him feel superior to her, at least for a few minutes or a few hours. High self-esteem—that is, a strong ongoing sense of knowing oneself as 'good enough'—and the ability to beat or violate an intimate are mutually exclusive. In other words, low self-esteem is a prerequisite for a person to be able to perceive a woman as an acceptable target for violence. It is only if we view ourselves as inadequate, inferior and unworthy can we view our chosen partner in the same light and behave violently towards that person.

RYAN'S MODEL OF 'MALE DYSFUNCTION'

Until this juncture, I have argued that low self-esteem characterises violent men, and that low self-esteem in males derives from father distance and the impossibility of achieving many masculine ideals. I have contended that there is a relationship between male low self-esteem and gender insecurity, and that this is exacerbated in boys by the inevitability of their perceiving themselves as having some 'female' qualities. This denial of female qualities, such as acknowledging feelings, when perpetuated into adult-hood, separates men from themselves. Low self-esteem is not related to male violence in a linear way, as not all men with low self-esteem are violent.

Gail Ryan *et al*[48] offer a cycle of dysfunction which culminates (but does not end) in sexual assault, exploitative personal rela-tions, vandalism and violence. She has devised this model to particularly explain the behaviour cycle of young male sex offen-ders. The Ryan dysfunctional cycle begins with poor self-esteem. The male feels bad about himself, perceiving himself to be re-jected, ignored, put-down, victimised, criticised, abandoned or controlled by others. This initial state is one of powerlessness. The second stage involves the expectation of rejection which is a reaction to these negative feelings. At this stage the perpetrator will behave in a way which will precipitate the feared rejection or he will reject the other person first to 'protect' himself. The former option may be carried out by picking a fight, making inappropriate approaches, being too controlling or by asking the impossible. The third stage (withdrawal) is a defence against the rejection he feared, which he precipitated either by rejecting or by picking on others.

During the fourth stage, his anger rises and he blames others for his anger and his feelings of rejection intermingle with his original bad feelings about himself.[49] This stage involves the perpetrator utilising fantasies of violent retaliation against the female or females.

> For all offenders, their fantasies compensate for the feelings of
> powerlessness...which triggered the cycle. The central theme is
> usually power and control, exaggerated in direct proportion to the
> level of personalization in the offender's interpretation of the incidents
> which triggered his...perceived rejection. The goal within the
> fantasies may be to evoke the same negative feelings in the victim by
> controlling, overpowering, defiling, and degrading.[50]

During the fifth stage the male plans violent retaliation. The rapist will often select, stalk and watch the woman he will assault. This is followed by the sixth stage in which he acts out the anger, the fantasies and/or the plan. 'For the less violent offender, the offence may be more exploitative and coercive but still fulfill the need for power and control. The offence vindicates the offen-der's feelings of rejection and makes him feel powerful'.[51] During the seventh stage, he rationalises the behaviour and minimises its seriousness. His feelings of power have passed and he now feels bad about himself or sorry for himself again. He may realise that his victim might die, she might leave him or she might lay charges against him.

The cycle is of course an 'ideal' cycle in that the seven phases will not necessarily be discrete and some phases may well not exist for many violent males. Stages four and five (the fantasies and the plans) probably do not exist as discrete stages for most batterers and would be nonexistent for chronic batterers. It is highly likely that they rapidly pass from stage four anger to stage six violence. The overall applicability of the schema derives from its comprehensive accounting for affective, behavioural and cognitive constituents of the violence.

THE RAMIFICATIONS OF HIGH EMOTIONAL DEPENDENCY

This male constellation of low self-esteem, high dependency and tenuous sense of masculinity appears to be paradigmatic for batterers, incest perpetrators and rapists.[52] I consider low self-esteem and a high level of dependency, against the general background of patriarchal social structures, to be necessary conditions for a male to batter a person with whom he is intimate. Low self-esteem allows one to perceive one's intimates as unworthy like oneself; high emotional dependency means that one has an extreme need for the affection of another person. This immediately places the insecure male in a contradictory situation. He knows at some level that he *must* have a partner, but he knows at the conscious level that 'real' men do not need others.[53] Thus the very need which he must fulfil to sustain himself is a sign that his masculinity is wanting.

The genesis of 'normal' levels of emotional dependence derives from the emotional economy inherent in the 'modern' family and contemporary child raising practices. Smacking children as a way of asserting parental authority and as a way of teaching children that some behaviours are forbidden or dangerous has been out of fashion recently, particularly in the literature on child abuse and wife battering. The child raising *modus operandi* that has become increasingly fashionable this century is that of parental emotional reward for 'good' behaviour and emotional withdrawal for 'bad' behaviour. This practice is perhaps more damaging for the child. What if parents are not familiar with the behavioural attributes of children at a given age and their expectations of the child are therefore unrealistic? Most of the child's behaviour is then deemed 'bad' and the child does not receive much positive affection, and under such circumstances the child's behaviour will become increasingly 'bad'. Emotional withholding by parents, particularly by fathers, has long-term consequences for the son.

Mark Poster claims that this way of child raising in the modern family is conducive to children's emotional dependence—in the first instance on the parents. Emotional dependence is an inability to feel emotionally whole without somebody else's emotional support. This may be healthy in a child, but if the condition survives to adulthood such people will tend to marry or form couples early in life because being alone is fraught with feelings of insecurity.

This very emotional dependence which is problematic in adulthood is an *a priori* of oedipal resolution and the development of the superego. The child's human need for love allows for the possibility of emotional dependence. The experience of being loved, along with frustration and desires, are the building blocks for superego formation. I postulate that insufficient unqualified love for any individual child (given the emotional economy), in combination with excessive frustration or insufficient frustration of desires, is conducive to an underdeveloped superego. By virtue of being violent, a deficient superego is indicated. If the superego were adequately developed, such behaviour would at least cause internal distress to the perpetrator. This is not so in many cases.

Hence we have the constellation—male positional identification, excessive emotional dependency needs and a defective superego. These factors derive from the emotionally distant father syndrome which sets up the basic condition of male positional identification. The batterer desperately needs a female partner, this very need sets up anxiety as he needs to prove his masculinity to himself and his dependency undermines that possibility. Thus she becomes the target of his violence emanating from his insecurity as a person and as a male.

Why will a 'loved' female be the likely target of all batterers and some rapists? Because of the capitalist-patriarchal role of women in our society. Women are responsible for emotional work in both the private and public domains, hence the preponderance of female nurses, social workers, kindergarten teachers, etc. The role of wife includes the responsibility for the emotional well being of her family, including that of her husband. A female partner is a necessity for an emotionally needy male. This woman will give him what he needs to make him feel whole. Of course such an anxiety-producing need is not always conscious, let alone articulated in a clear fashion. These expectations, this fantasy, this emotional hunger, cannot be satisfied by any 'normal' human. His needs are so great that his partner will inevitably 'fail' him—as he perceives it. She will not be a good enough wife. Many battering men list in detail to their wives their multiple deficiencies as wife, mother and housekeeper.

As well as bringing unconscious unrealistic emotional expectations to the partnership, the very nature of the husband-wife dyad in our present-day families has an intensity that such a male will find difficult to manage. The characteristics which distinguish marriage or relationships from others are intimacy, sexual activities and often the expectation that the relationship will last for a long time. Intimate relations in relationships, in combination with frequent interactions, total personality involvement and inevitable conflicts of interest, can easily produce hostility. Intimate relations in combination with frequent interactions and total personality involvement also simultaneously produce a fear of relationship dissolution and resultant suppression of hostility.[54] Thus marriage, especially for those with high emotional dependence, is a hotbed of contradictions.

The young adult male has a desire to meet his unacknowledged dependency needs by becoming half of a couple. However this experience of intimacy is likely to raise anxieties about regression, mostly unconsciously. Hence he has a fear of intimacy as well as a need for it. What does intimacy involve? Intimacy (in this discussion) is an emotional closeness between two people. Recognition of, and acceptance of, one's so-called 'positive' and 'negative' feelings in response to people and situations are steps towards intimacy. Then the person needs to be able to express these feelings in an accessible and acceptable way so that another can recognise them. The second person in turn needs to be able to more or less read the messages accurately, and that person must also recognise her/his own affective responses, accept them and communicate them. Many studies have shown that men are less emotionally expressive than women.[55] Men's self-disclosure is more likely to be cognitive and activity or interest-centred rather than affective. Men are found to be less empathic than women.[56]

This fits in well with the male gender stereotypes—there is no mention of expressivity, affectivity or empathy, in fact the stereotype is that males are 'unemotional'. If this were true, men's lives would be quite simple. However emotion is intrinsic to the human condition. Men whose gender identification is positional know that males do not show their feelings. If feelings are not expressed they do not go away—in fact they are inevitably manifested directly or indirectly. The more indirect the expression, the less intelligible the message.

Another aspect of intimacy is physical closeness. Herb Goldberg believes that:

> Adult males have profound defences against touching; their reactions border on being phobic [an irrational fear]. They can hardly bear to be touched by other men and being touched by women is perceived as a prelude to sex... The male hero images of our culture are the 'untouchables'—cold, self-contained.[57]

Thus the male whose gender identification is positional is also anxious in physical proximity with others, unless it is male backslapping or associated with female sexual activity.

> To win, to be superior, to be successful, to conquer—all demonstrate masculinity... And it would be surprising if these notions of masculinity did not find expression in men's sexual behaviour. Indeed, sex may be the arena where these notions of masculinity are most intensely played out, particularly by men who feel powerless in the rest of their lives, and hence, whose masculinity is threatened by his sense of powerlessness.[58]

Sexual expression is not an inherent aspect of intimacy or *vice versa*, but commonly the two overlap. In particular, emotional or intimacy difficulties may manifest themselves indirectly in sexual relations. That male batterers and rapists have sexual problems is borne out by a small number of studies.[59]

As most information about male batterers was gleaned from their female victims in the earlier years of renewed social concern about male violence, so most information about male batterers' sexuality has derived from battered females. In the late 1970s, the Battered Women Research Centre at Colorado investigated the lives of 400 battered women.[60] Lenore Walker presented some of this data to several American congressional committees and the United States Commission on Civil Rights. A range of questions on sex were interspersed amongst other questions. A non-battered control group was also studied.

The results of this study revealed that 59 per cent of the women were forced to have sex with the batterer, in contrast to 7 per cent with non-batterers; 41 per cent of women were asked to perform 'unusual' sex acts (such as bondage, or with animals) with the battering partners, as against 5 per cent with the non-battering partner. Consequently 85 per cent of the women with violent husbands viewed sex as 'unpleasant' compared with 29 per cent of the women with non-violent husbands. Of these, 43 per cent related the unpleasantness with force. Almost half of the men *and* women in the battering relationships withheld sex in order to 'get what they wanted'. In the nonviolent relationships, 11 per cent of men and 16 per cent of women did so.[61]

I believe that one of the main reasons a man chooses a wife or female partner is so that he has guaranteed sexual relations with her. He could sexually satisfy himself by masturbation or by sexual activities with other men. In general, in our society, no doubt for complex reasons, men are discouraged from seriously considering these options in the long term. Hence a wife is seen as the salve of her husband's sexual needs as well as his emotional needs. Where emotional dependency is frightening, this need will most likely be denied and become, in the husband's mind, merely the need for sexual gratification. However, since there is a sexual-dependency built into the relationship too, even this aspect of marital intimacy has the potential to be disturbing to an insecure male. Furthermore, his need to see himself as a masculine sexual being can depend on her response to him sexually. Again, too much may be implicitly expected of her. It is her job to make him 'feel like a man' and if, in his eyes, she fails to do this, he may attack her. Vic Seidler honestly acknowledges that men:

> end up attempting to fulfil a whole range of separate...needs in our sexual contact...since the very recognition of needs compromises our masculine control, we seek to satisfy our different needs without really being able to identity them...We can blame our partners for not being ready to interpret our needs for us.[62]

Why is there a connection in some males between sex and violence? It may be that the low self-esteem, highly dependent male blurs sex and intimacy. Intimacy with its closeness and confusion of you–me may be a fearful state for such men. Thus violence may be one way they attempt to distance their female partner, so as to feel safer and in control of her and implicitly of themselves. Rape could be a variation on the same theme: intimacy is feared so rape in a way is safe sex wherein the feelings of closeness are kept at bay by terrorising a female target. Child sexual assault within the family may also work for the perpetrator partly at this level: the male can feel emotionally safe and distant by having sex with a female who is not an adult, who can be manipulated and sworn to secrecy and over whom he has tremendous power.

Males often depend on their female partners for emotional nurturance and sexual sustenance. Hence fears of being personally incomplete and sexually insecure are intensified. These circumstances describe the battering male and are expressed by his personal possessiveness of his partner and his unfounded sexual jealousy in relation to her. Jealousy is amongst the most frequently cited characteristics of the male batterer.[63] The severity of the possessiveness and jealousy was made abundantly clear to Bruce Rounsaville:

> Seventy-seven percent of the women rated their husbands as 'very possessive', citing such behaviour as calling up the woman numerous times daily while he was at work to insure that she was at home or insisting on accompanying her even on small errands outside the home, in order to prevent a possible rendezvous with another man. This possessiveness was not limited to sexual jealousy in that many of the women stated that their partners prevented visits to the home by female friends or relatives and abused them if they attempted to visit their friends or relatives at their homes.[64]

Clinicians who work with such men are compelled to comment on the extreme possessiveness and jealousy and note its bizarreness and inappropriateness. However they do not seem to appreciate the powerful needs underlying such behaviours. If a batterer's wife continues a friendship with other people, he feels that he may not have her when he needs her, he is afraid that others may be more interesting than him and he feels *he has lost a part of himself* when she is with other people. If his wife talks to another man, is looked at by another man, let alone has sex with another man, his masculinity is in question; his wife may pander to another man's need to feel male, and if she did have sex with somebody else *his sexual identity would be lost.*

The proximity to another person inherent in heterosexual relationships is also fertile ground for projection. If a battering male feels incomplete without his wife's total attention, it will obviously be difficult for him to know which parts of the dyad are him and which are her. This is the 'bonding' or blurred boundaries of which some case historians speak.[65] The confusion of 'him' and 'her' may result in his accusing her of sexual infidelity because *he* has other sexual partners.Some of the literature on male batterers confirms that it is the batterer who is sexually promiscuous, and it is the batterer who fears his wife's sexual promscuity and accuses her of being so without any evidence whatsoever. His promiscuity could be related to the fact that having sex with one woman does not sufficiently assure his sense of masculinity and maybe more than one woman will. Also, spreading his sexual activities amongst a number of women may help diminish the emotional intensity often associated with monogamous sex, and the ensuing fears that this raises.

A further aspect of the 'married couple' situation which can add to the emotional discomfort of an insecure male is simply that physical proximity in an unstructured way over time will produce an array of unpredictable feelings. The male gender stereotype does not acknowledge that men experience feelings, recognise them or deal with them in any constructive way. Thus the male is unprepared for his emotional reactions within a couple or a family relationship, and he has had little opportunity to practise recognising various emotions and dealing with them in a productive fashion. Such a male may well feel that, internally, he is 'out of control', and this will be a state which creates great anxiety in emotion-denying males. One paradoxical way in which people who feel out of control attempt to cope with it is by controlling other people and other things. Some male batterers are considered to be extremely 'controlling' of their partners.[66] This controlling is an abuse of the unequal power structure within marriage and it can have an emotional substrate. These controlling batterers take control to the extreme; they determine their wives' every activity and check to ensure that she has done all they have told her and in the manner demanded.

5 | What can be done to prevent male violence towards females in our society

In the previous chapters I have detailed the aspects of patriarchal social structures, the modern family, male gender construction and male personal attributes which contribute to the construction of violent males. The first three factors are necessary foundations in our society, and the last cluster of factors make the difference between a male who has the potential to be violent towards females and one who is highly likely to do so. The traits of low self-esteem and high emotional dependence are the sufficient conditions which tip the scales. However, these characteristics cannot be dissociated from the structural factors from which they arise. If our society were to decide that violence by men towards women is totally unacceptable and that it is our first priority to eradicate such practices, we could not do so until *all* of the contributory factors were changed. For primary prevention of male violence, interventions at the structural level of society are imperative.

Male violence towards females is not pathological as such, rather it is one manifestation of the contradictions of our class structures and gender structures. Being violent is not 'normal' either. Because it can emerge so easily from complex 'normal' social structural interactions and because the contradictions that males actively live are intensifying, a higher rate of male violence is likely over the next few generations unless major social changes take place. Thus my approach encompasses both macro-social structural aspects of the problem and male personality characteristics emanating from modern family structures and processes. At the secondary and tertiary levels of prevention and intervention, violent men must take responsibility for their own violence. This means that individual men are responsible; so are those who accept male violence as a fact of life (albeit perpetrated by 'others'); and so are male laws, values, structures and practices which encourage male violence or fail to strongly censure male violence. Hence, as with many researchers who make suggestions with regard to social change to expedite the abolition of violence against women[1], I begin with patriarchy.

SOCIAL POLICY IMPLICATIONS DERIVING FROM PATRIARCHAL SOCIAL STRUCTURES

Sexual equality for women and men at work and in marriage.

Whilst women do not actually have employment opportunities equal to those of men, men can utilise their material superiority to take advantage of women in a multiplicity of ways. Whilst women's pay is less than men's for comparable work[2], men can equate their superior earning power to superior privileges within marriage. Marriage itself must be a contract of equals with equivalent responsibilities and privileges. If marriage is an equal arrangement, no husband can resort to the 'I'm the head of the household' defence for interfering with his wife's rights. If men and women see themselves in charge of their negotiated roles, rights and responsibilities, it can be clear within intimate partnerships that violence is not an acceptable part of the relationship. And the quality of life, practically and emotionally, gained by working towards equality can outweigh feared losses associated with changed social–sexual relations.

Sexual equality between men and women means that there is no place for male violence against females in any of its forms: battering, rape[3], sexual harassment or viewing women as sex objects. Physical violence, sexual violence, emotional violence, verbal put-downs and anti-female 'jokes' are not behaviours appropriate for men who respect themselves and their partners, mothers and daughters. Equality also excludes the notion that men have the right to own and sexually possess, violate or control women and children (male and female). Incest is at one end of this sexual violence continuum, wherein a male owns his children and may privately use and abuse them for his own emotional, sexual and power needs without any acknowledgement of his children's basic human (but unforthcoming) rights.

Accessible, adequate and affordable child care centres for the benefit of men and women who do not choose to be full-time parents.

The patriarchal notions that parenting equals mothering and that men are not responsible for children must be eradicated. Whilst men see child raising as women's work, they do not take responsibility for the fact that they are parents. Whilst men abrogate their parental and child raising responsibilities, they can force the mothers of their children to stay at home, to mother or to search for possible child care options. Thus, occasional care, after school care, vacation care and work-based care facilities need to be expanded. The unequal gendered division of responsibilities results in men having superior financial, social and political resources in comparison to women at home with children, without economic independence or public sphere privileges.

Active parenting by fathers.

As well as denying women access to the labour market and exacerbating material dependency on the father of their children, these lopsided parenting arrangements set up tendencies for children to be deprived of adequate nurturance by, and access to, adult men. Sole responsibility for parenting by one adult is often fraught with difficulties for both the adult and the children. The social isolation, the emotional intensity and the onerous responsibility are circumstances that are conducive to burnout and fear of failure. That most mothers do not succumb to such stresses is a testimony to their valiant efforts to place the needs of the child first and alleviate as best they can these conditions which are built into most child raising circumstances at the present time.

Fathering can begin at birth and paternity leave can allow him the opportunity to develop skills with the baby (as the mother has to) which can be confidence building. Men can be active parents of their children and men must share the responsibility of finding non-family alternatives if both parents decide such resources are needed. Imagine the priority child care centres would have if all male politicians, businessmen and professionals suddenly had to look after their children for six months during the working year! If men took their fatherhood seriously, they would care about the (unpaid) working conditions of their wives and the practical and emotional environments of their children and endeavour to change these circumstances.

The physical and emotional distance of the father from his sons is a key factor in male positional identification, which sets the sons up for difficulties with their personal and gender identities. I have not discussed the significance of father inaccessability regarding daughters, but I am sure daughters would gain from father involvement too. The father can also achieve a richer personal life through emotional engagement with his children. In my opinion, it is father distance in the modern family more than any other factor at the present time which makes the 'normal' family conducive to low self-esteem and gender insecurity in sons. This tendency is exacerbated by the general social practice of deeming parents (often meaning mothers) as totally responsible for child raising. Hence the extended family and the rest of the community believe it is not in their interest, or their responsibility, to care for children in general.

Thus parenting in our society is at the extreme end of a possible continuum—that is only one or two adults who are responsible for raising children. If children were parented by neighbours, child care workers, friends and relatives, as well as parents, they would have access to a greater range of interactions, more potential for being loved and feeling lovable and a variety of role models. I am not advocating the 'destruction' of the family, but I am pointing out that children and society can gain from children's greater access to numbers of caring adults. The return—emotionally, practically and with regard to time investment—of the father to the role of active parent has considerable advantages for the children, for the father, for the mother and for society. Active parenting by fathers from childbirth facilitates mutual attachment of father and baby, and some researchers deem such processes are conducive to prevention of male physical and sexual violence against their own child. It may also decrease female violence towards children.

A guaranteed minimum income above poverty levels should be provided by the government to all active parents in the form of supporting parent benefit or unemployment benefit.

The purpose of this policy is to ensure that the dire straits of poverty do not exacerbate any violent tendencies a male may have; and to guarantee any female with children who needs to leave an unsatisfactory relationship that she can do so without jeopardising their needs for food, shelter and clothing. Single parents who receive a supporting parent benefit should be allowed to take a part-time job and earn *any* amount of income on top of the benefit. Some single parents get caught in a poverty trap by keeping their earnings low enough to retain the full benefit and nonfinancial advantages attached to it. Single parents are raising members of our society's next generation. Of all active parents, they need to be able to afford child care services for the benefit of their children as well as their own economic and emotional wellbeing.

Unemployment benefits should not be paid to the couple as a

unit—they should be paid to both individuals. If there are children in the family and the father is not an active (at least half-
time) parent, then the mother could be the designated applicant
and recipient of the benefit. I do not believe for a moment that
such a situation will come about in our society in the near future:
'What—a man dependent on his wife for the dole!' My intention
in the suggestion is that married women with children in the
lowest income group should not be less equal than their husbands
because of unemployment. It is well known that the majority of
unemployed males contribute minimally more—and sometimes
less—to parenting activities than they did when they worked full
time.[4]

*Cheap public housing should be readily available to families with
low incomes, with a first priority for single-parent families and a
second priority for poor two-parent families with children
under 17 years of age.*

One of the problems associated with the present refuge focus in
the approach to battered women is where they can afford to go
after the refuge? They need to have access to cheap public housing and have top priority in applying for and gaining it. Affordable housing must be available for any parent who does not wish
to remain in a difficult or violent marital relationship.[5] Publicly
provided housing needs to be available immediately to families in
crisis. In this case, either the mother or the father may leave the
family home with some, none or all of the children.

When both parents in a family with young children are unemployed, they need to know that if they cannot afford to keep their
present home there is publicly provided housing which will decrease their expenditure on rent and enable them to afford food
and other basics. Again this policy is to ensure that male lower
income earners are not forced towards battering as a possible
'coping' mechanism by virtue of poverty. Housing priorities
should be for families with young children. Greater provision of
public housing overall is therefore required.

*The media should discourage war-mongering and approval of
violence particularly in children's television programmes.
Legislation should be enacted for these purposes if media owners
do not agree to monitoring and decreasing the exposure of
children to violent 'entertainment'.*

Violence against women cannot be dealt with entirely as a discrete activity outside the violent social context within which we

live. The 'taste' for violence as entertainment, news and excitement has been encouraged and promoted over the last 25 years. This 'taste' can also be discouraged. *Straw Dogs* and *A Clockwork Orange* shocked us in the mid 1960s, and the violence was rationalised as being part of the 'meaning' and 'creativity' of the films. Now violence as entertainment is commonplace and one or two generations of children have grown up with a continuing supply of visual violence in their lounge room. Television companies know that young children are awake until, say, 9.00 p.m., but 'children's' programmes cease at 6.30 p.m. All television programmes which run until at least 9.00 p.m. should provide a greater proportion of shows in which violence is neither the medium nor the message.[6] Children's programmes need to be scrutinised more closely as many of them involve killing as a means to a 'good' end. The more realistic and interpersonal the violence is, the more readily children perceive it as part of their lives. A cartoon story of St George slaying the dragon is more akin to fantasy than are boys fighting against each other or being abducted by threatening male adults.

Television is particularly important as most homes have one, it is frequently turned on and its visual nature reduces every act to a concrete and explicit one. Books are perhaps less of a concern as the visual images are static and less realistic than those on television. Radio is also less worrisome as the child is left to create her/his own images as the words pass by. Television news is particularly problematic as violence from every part of the world is *ipso facto* news. Newsreaders should be encouraged to comment on the sadness or distress associated with specific news items, instead of recounting the details with mechanical voices. The absence of disapproval of violence is akin to the approval of violence. This is a daily, if not hourly, television occurrence with virtually no anti-violence promotion.

Values which are child-appreciating and promoting of caring need to be encouraged in adults and children.

It is insufficient to legislate *against* the promotion or acceptance of violence; our society has to promote positive practices and attitudes which engender loving, caring and nurturance. Perhaps at this stage of our history it is easier in our society to be violent and achieve 'success' than it is to be loving and achieve 'success'. Loving does not come 'naturally'. The view that women could love naturally came from generations of women raising female children to nurture so that the end result looked natural. Children *learn* to love in their family and only parents who actively express their love teach the skills. This is part of the so called 'cycle of violence' or 'intergenerational transmission' explanation of wife battering or child abuse. Not only do violent families easily perpetuate violence, but if pro-violence is combined with non-loving the inability to love is perpetuated too. The latter may well be the more important of the two.

Our society needs to promote loving qualities in men and women. Men who produce pulp movies for television should take up the challenge of portraying men as caring people without making a joke of them, dressing them up as women or allocating them to a fringe culture. Men in reality are more caring and loving than they are portrayed in the media. Why are rich and successful film producers afraid to imitate, create or encourage roles of caring males?

Child-appreciating aspects of our society are even more hidden than our awareness of men's capacity to love. Lots of parents love their children and appreciate their spontaneity, openness and energy. Children are rarely an integral part of mainstream film or theatre and when they are their positive attributes are not often celebrated. Adults, other than parents, women and close relatives, are not encouraged to interact with children. In this respect our society is as much ageist (at the younger as well as the older end of the continuum) as it is sexist. Adults can gain from spending time with children just as children can gain from adult interest and appreciation.

One of the reasons that children are not valued in our society is that 'worth' is measured; and the common measure we have for it is wealth, possessions and income. Men have absorbed this ideology more thoroughly than women because they have been income earners at the expense of being fathers. We need to develop an appreciation of caring people and an appreciation of children to allow the next generation to care for and appreciate children and know that these are worthy skills and values. Men who feel comfortable developing their expressive and caring skills will not violate and demean their wives; men who appreciate and value children will not undermine them by neglecting them or abusing them; and men who care for and appreciate themselves will do neither. Men who actively value the sharing of intimacy and sensuality are not rapists or incest perpetrators.

Professionals who work with individuals, couples and families need to be made aware of the realities of domestic violence and factors which contribute to it—particularly the patriarchal assumptions of their own profession which prevent dealing with family victims of male violence in a constructive manner.

During their training or studentship these workers (who include police, lawyers, doctors, psychologists, nurses, and social workers) should be educated about the extent, seriousness and ramifications of wife battering, rape and incest, as well as referral possibilities. The majority of young adults entering these professions are single and may have fanciful views about marriage and intimate relationships which have not been tested out. Naivety and ignorance are not helpful for the workers and they are dangerous for both the violated and the violator.

In their preparatory courses, such professionals need to be familiarised with the difficulties inherent in forming a relationship and in parenting. Their emotional responses to family violence need to be acknowledged and worked through. I suspect that many of the paternalistic, distant and moralising reactions battered wives and rape victims receive are due to the naive, unprepared and inexperienced workers' outrage, fear, horror, anger and similar emotions. These are normal responses, but they will be expressed directly or indirectly to the client unless they are dealt with before they arise in practice. Workers need to be clear about what they believe to be ethically unacceptable behaviour. If we are to eradicate wife battering and rape, I expect no police officer, lawyer, doctor, nurse or social worker to merely accept any such behaviour. This does not mean that they should moralise or be disparaging, but the violence should be acknowledged and be acknowledged as unacceptable. The premises from which men who work with batterers begin is that the behaviour is unacceptable, the batterer is responsible, it must stop and he will require help to stop it.

Wife battering, rape and incest must be actively criminalised. This criminalisation should then be enforced by the police and the law. Males as responsible people should voice their disapproval of such crimes.

Assault of a wife by her husband must be recognised as criminal assault, not only by the law but by the public in general, spouses, the police and members of the legal profession. Police and lawyers must be seen to act upon the law and enforce it. If men have been assaulting their wives under the protection of the marriage licence, the fact that such an activity is now a criminal offence will not stop them. They may become even more controlling, and prevent their wives from having necessary medical treatment and threaten them with further violence if they tell even their closest friend. Men should be informed by the media that the police are arresting such assailants and charging them appropriately. Women need to be aware that such men are being charged with criminal offences so that they too do not believe that the marriage licence protects men.

Not only must such men be charged with assault, but the public needs to know that solicitors and magistrates take the charges seriously and fine them a sizeable amount of money or jail them. Some may argue that this will make an angry man angrier. This may well be so for some batterers, however such men need to learn that their behaviour is unacceptable to their wife, the police and lawyers. If the professionals involved exempt the batterer from the teeth of the law, he learns that representatives of the law are toothless. They excuse him on the grounds that he may hurt his wife more; and his wife learns that not only is she powerless to do anything about the assaults, but so is the machinery of the law. Would a magistrate fail to fine another assailant on the grounds that he might be even more angry towards his neighbour whom he assaulted? It is important for both the battered person and the batterer that somebody (the police) or some institution (the law) can resist the batterer's behaviour. They must say 'no' to battering, and show that they are *not afraid* to do so. Many violent men are actually afraid of what they might do in the future. If the police do not utilise their powers, if legislation is not made to work and his victim cannot gain protection, the batterer rightly assumes that they are afraid of him. This ironically does not make aggressive men feel safer. If such 'forces' as the police and lawyers are fearful of him, his fears about the future are intensified. The batterer has not been able to set adequate limits for himself. The law must set limits for him and punish him if he transgresses.

Legislation which deals with domestic violence must be publicised and explained in newspapers and on television. People must know that wife battering and rape are criminal acts. Each of us must be able to say to ourselves that male violence against females is a crime and such behaviour is unacceptable, no matter what 'extenuating' circumstances. Some battered women cannot speak up because they recognise their friends' silence as tacit acceptance. Some batterers and rapists feel they have more support for their actions than they do if nobody actually says that it is unacceptable.[7] It is the responsibility of all of us to say 'no' to violence against women. Men who are concerned about violence can join women and voice their disapproval of wife battering, so that it cannot be perceived as a norm by virtue of men's resounding silence.

Men's consciousness-raising (CR) groups can be established by men who are concerned about the adverse aspects of patriarchy at the macro-social level and in their own lives.

Such groups are being established, or continue to exist, mostly in cities and usually with small numbers of men actively participating. The fact that some men are expending energy mobilising other men, are willing to share their learning and facilitating skills and share their feelings, is an important positive counteraction to all of the bad news we hear about men. These groups have a brief to support each other in ways that men are quite unused to; and to confront each other appropriately, firmly and constructively. As Connell says of feminist CR groups, they can 'disrupt the taken-for-grantedness of many...practices'.[8] The consciousness-raising, to be effective, needs to be both cognitive and affective. Just talking about problems will not change awareness—participants need to be emotionally involved. This may well be the greatest challenge for such groups. Since the male has been poorly prepared for intimacy with men or women, and behaviours with both genders are ritualised, developing a trusting environment in which men can display emotion will require hard work and determination.

Men in such groups must eventually confront each other and themselves regarding such profound issues as power, sexuality, responsibility and insecurity. Feminists such as Stevi Jackson clearly relate gendered power inequalities to male violence towards females.

> Sexual relationships are built around sexual inequalities, are scripted for actors where roles have been predefined as subordinate and superordinate, and hence involve the exercise of power which may be manifested in the sexual act itself, as well as in other aspects of the relationship. Rape, then, is simply an extreme manifestation of our culturally accepted patterns of male-female relationship.[9]

Wife battering, rape and incest all emerge from patriarchal powers that are passed on from one generation to the next inexplicitly and are therefore difficult to scrutinise. These acts against females are also informed by sexuality and gender, conveniently confused with each other. The power and sex at a personal level are frequently disowned, dissociated, denied. Men must work towards being responsible for their sexual acts and abuses of power. Whilst it is socially acceptable for men to blame their partners for their own violence, for men to blame rape victims for their own violence, and for men to blame children for their own violence, the violence in our world will not diminish. Men collectively need to grow up and take responsibility for themselves and their actions. If men continue to assume social rights and abrogate social responsibility, the cycles of violence will continue to be perpetuated.

Whilst we have wife battering in our society, viable secondary prevention measures must be accessible to women and men. Battered women, rape and incest victims need to have ready access to legal, welfare and financial information, refuges and women's support groups. Violent men who want to change need to be aware of the services which deal specifically with these problems.

The main issues here are that female victims of male violence must have interventions and information, and refuges must be available to them. Such resources need to continue to be expanded.

Where do battering men stand? Some believe they have a right to assault their wives and they have no feelings of remorse about their actions. Such men must be dealt with actively and thoroughly by the police and the law. Others may suspect that their behaviour is not the norm and not acceptable, they may feel guilty at times and they may know that it is now a criminal offence. If any batterers are in such circumstances they are trapped. Willpower alone will not stop most battering, just as it will not stop most cigarette smokers who decide to stop smoking the first time. They need skilled assistance. Hence more groups for violent men need to be established by nonviolent men, and their availability publicised.[10] Education and preparation for such work needs to be provided by the state, as we have so few male professionals with these skills. Amateurs may exacerbate the problems.

SOCIAL POLICY IMPLICATIONS DERIVING FROM MODERN FAMILY PRACTICES

School-aged children of both genders need to be educated to develop skills in communication, assertiveness, problem solving and conflict resolution.

The development of communication skills and assertiveness skills begins early in childhood. As part of personal development courses beginning in early primary school, children should be encouraged to express their feelings, listen to others and share their successes and difficulties. The only way to develop these skills is to practise them. At a later stage the principles of assertiveness can be taught and children can learn to differentiate aggression and passivity from assertiveness. They can practise saying what they want without putting anyone else down and without thinking that they have less right to ask for something than others do. Ideally this should be done with small mixed groups of boys and girls so that both genders experience each others' similarities and practise respecting each other. This needs to be begun at an early age because some older primary school children have entrenched gender prejudices and they may sabotage the exercises and not gain any personal (or even intellectual) insights that come from practising and experiencing meaningful communication.

Problem-solving skills can be built on to communication and assertiveness skills. By developing experience in these domains, children are allowed to realise the normalcy of conflict within families, friendships, classrooms, etc. Thus conflict is not hidden or denied. Fear of conflict is diminished even if children are only taught that conflict can be dealt with and that something useful may emerge from it. At present many families consider conflict to be dangerous and believe it can only come to a 'bad' end. Under these circumstances, family members contort their communications on certain issues and it looks as if they are not in conflict, but the very fact that it is suppressed usually means that the anger and resentments manifest in some distorted way. If children are aware of the inevitability of conflict and are not afraid of possible consequences, they are more likely to deal with problems openly and constructively.

Violent men commonly have poor communication skills, are nonassertive, deny conflict and may provoke conflict but will not discuss it or deal with it productively. The more skills in this area a young child develops, the more likely they will use them and gain even further skills. It is the noncommunicative and the nonassertive children who do not practise and do not gain competence who will have recourse to aggressive or passive behaviours. The more assertive children we raise, there will be less need to resort to violence as a problem-solving tactic and the less need for others to passively accept this *modus operandi*.

School-aged children of both genders would benefit from developing skills in preparation for caring for children.

This is not necessarily heterosexist or pronatalist—the aims are to encourage children to understand the basics of child development, the needs of babies and young children and to develop skills to 'handle' babies. Children in the middle primary school years have the cognitive skills to learn about the normal development of the foetus, the baby and the preschool and infant school child. The physical and emotional needs and development can be dealt with together so that the children do not learn that one is more important than the other or that they are separable.

Both genders can ideally attend these classes together so that teachers can be seen to support the notion that child care skills are necessary for the development of males and females. An excellent example of a programme run along these lines by teachers and nurses in Western Australia is detailed in *A Guide Book for Teaching Parenting*[11] and is offered to more than 8000 year 9 boys and girls every year. Male teachers with such knowledge and skills would be good role models for primary school boys who have already learnt in their family that fathers do not look after children. Infant and preschool siblings could come to the classroom to allow children without younger siblings to see them, handle them, ask questions about them and talk with them. As with communication skills, which cannot be improved without practice, baby handling skills cannot be miraculously achieved by thoroughly unprepared parents at the birth of a child. This information would counterbalance the baby image which is portrayed on television. Babies are not only pristine, smiling, arm-waving bundles of delight. They defecate, scream, dribble and get red in the face. Children need not approach their fertile years in ignorance of babies and basic child development processes.

Men will not be well prepared to handle babies if boys are not taught some basic child care skills.[12] Fathers will not feel comfortable with their offspring unless they feel that it is their job to be with them and that they are as well prepared (or as ill prepared) as mothers. If fathers are not informed about babies and feel uncomfortable about them they will not share parenting, and if they are forced to share parenting they will not do a good job. Men need to feel willing and able to take up an active parenting role to break this monopoly of mothering that our society has intensified to the ultimate detriment of children, mothers and fathers. Preparing children for the possibility of becoming child carers does not prevent male violence directly but provides possibilities for the next generation of men and women to aim for more egalitarian relationships and an awareness of parenting as a challenging but demanding job with only some rewards.

School aged children of both genders need to be educated to expect to work to earn a living and to help support their partner and children should they have any in the future.

This could involve a series of discussions and values-clarification exercises. The main aim of this aspect of the personal development course is to not set boys up to believe that they alone must earn the income and support dependents. Girls also must not be set up to believe that they are entitled to be supported by a male partner whether they have children or not. If girls can learn to question this idea of entitlement, they may take their education and careers more seriously. Many middle-aged women who are working full time did not expect to be doing so. If young women realise that they may be employees for a long time, their expectations of work and themselves can change.

Boys can adapt to the notion that they do not have to face the onerous responsibility of supporting a family alone, just as girls can be allowed to realise that they do not have to face the onerous responsibility of raising children alone. And boys and girls must be prepared attitudinally, with information and with basic skills both for the workplace and for the home. Boys may then grow up knowing that they can be valued by themselves, by their peers and by women for themselves, not for the money that they earn or the status of the job that they do. Money is not a measure of masculinity.

Income can drop and statuses can change. Girls and boys also need to be prepared for the possibility of unemployment—the rate of unemployment has increased over the last three decades and will probably continue to do so. Some children will find themselves amongst the ranks of the unemployed for years of their adult lives. Both genders need to be informed about unemployment and the general factors associated with it. They need to know that they have not caused it and it is not their fault that they are 'unemployable'.

Preparing young people of both genders for the likelihood of employment and the possibility of unemployment may not directly prevent male violence. However it does prepare the next generation to have realistic expectations about work. The argument that men displace their economic frustrations onto their wives loses its potential as an excuse[13] if women too feel responsible for earning an income and neither partner blames or resents the other for unemployment. Shared paid work and parenting is more conducive to equal rights and responsibilities in both the public and domestic domains.

School-aged children of both genders can be educated about the realities of sex, establishing long-term emotional relationships and parenting.

According to Jackson:

> Learning about sex in our society involves learning about guilt, indeed children learn taboos associated with sexuality before they are made aware of the scripts within which they operate. The association between sex and dirtiness is still with us despite the so-called 'sexual revolution' and our supposedly 'permissive' society. Children still learn about sex through dirty jokes and whispered clandestine secrets and find the taboo nature of sexuality confirmed by the evasive or negative attitudes of adults towards it.[14]

That this is the case reveals to me that many parents have not become sexually adult or responsible. This cycle of ignorance, embarrassment, bravado and self-righteous moralising has to be whittled away.

Adults as parents and schoolteachers can overtly prepare children of the next generation for some of the realities of sexual relations and intimacy in our society. Information is vital. So is the scrutiny of values and beliefs and fantasies young adults have regarding such topics as contraception, sex, love, marriage, homosexuality, masturbation, AIDS and babies. To counter the *status quo*, boys must be urged to take responsibility for their fertility and for their sexual practices[15] and question their perceived right to pressure others for sexual service. Girls must be urged to take responsibility for their own health and wellbeing by refusing to participate in sexual activities and contraceptive use which interferes with this wellbeing.

Just as it is a fantasy for many men to expect that they will become rich, famous and admired by virtue of their career trajectory, so it is a fantasy for many women to expect that they will be loved, satisfied and rewarded by virtue of their mothering and 'wifely' skills. If men can come undone by judging their own worth by their income, so women can come undone by judging their own worth by their parenting, their wifeliness and the cleanliness of their home. Both are setting standards that are intrinsically difficult to achieve. Unrealistic expectations of marriage are a prescription for failure and some men respond to such circumstances by behaving violently.

Boys and girls need to de-mystify the glamour, excitement and inevitability of marriage as portrayed in the media. Marriages are complex, mostly unwritten, contracts. As no other contract is expected to cure our problems and satisfy all of our emotional, practical and sexual needs, neither will marriage.[16] The problems we take into a long-term relationship will remain with us and resurface in unpredictable ways. Emotional and practical needs cannot be satisfied by only one person; and sexual satisfaction for both parties is not guaranteed by marriage.

Marriage is not an end; if anything it is a beginning. Marriage is not a cure-all—both partners have to work at dealing with the difficulties inherent in it. Ongoing sexual relationships are not an escape; they constitute a confrontation with another and with one-self. Marriage, as with the families from which we emerged, is con-flict ridden. *Emotional partnerships are intrinsically conflictual.* There is no need for any young person to expect that his or her mar-riage will not be. Because young people *want* a better marriage than their parents, this will not eventuate through wishful thinking. A viable marriage can only come from two mature people putting time, energy and affection into it.

Marriage does not have to be an assumed childhood aim. A more appropriate childhood aim could be self-sustenance. If young adults can appreciate the achievements of finding a job, leaving home and running a viable household of any kind they choose, that can be an excellent aim. Young adults who have experienced this autonomy and success know that they can look after themselves and get by in the world. If they wish to choose marriage later, they have already passed through the rites of passage involved in leaving their family of origin and they come as comparatively independent adults to marriage. The opportu-nity to experience being responsible for day-to-day household activities such as paying the rent, shopping and cooking will pre-pare young adults for some of the practical tasks of living in our society.

Parent education programmes and other personal development programmes should continue in high school after the foundations have been built in primary school. High school is too late to begin these courses, particularly for boys, as many have concluded already that communication, babies and marriage are not for them. However sex *is* for them, and even though babies and marriage are not necessary consequences, frequently enough they are. So with boys in particular we need to inform them well in primary school and offer them skills to further their knowledge and thinking about these issues in high school. Without adequate knowledge of the skills and energy demanded by present-day parenting, parents of both genders can set themselves up for frustrations and failures which may contribute to violence.

Two significant aspects of child raising need to be broached in parent education classes. The first is that hitting is not the only, the first or the most frequently utilised method of 'teaching' a child. The second is that withdrawal of affection should not be the only, the first or most frequently utilised method of 'teaching' a child. In my opinion the second method should never be used and the first method only occasionally. The dangers associated with the withdrawal of affection as punishment for wrong doing is that the basic lesson the child learns is that their parent(s) do not love them unless things are done 'properly'. All children must inevitably do many things inadequately or improperly.

What all children need is unconditional love, that is, they need to feel loved for themselves. This does not mean they are given emotional (or any other) rewards for 'bad' behaviour or that 'bad' behaviour is condoned. Inappropriate behaviour is disapproved of and sanctioned against in some way, but not by withdrawal of affection even by one parent. Privileges or treats can easily be withheld. The child's difficult behaviour must be separated from the child's sense of being a person. Hence the child remains loved but specific behaviours are 'punished' or sanctioned against. The expression of anger, annoyance and disapproval by a parent as a reaction to certain behaviours is natural but it is not the same as withdrawal of affection. Expression of disapproval, frustration or anger need not be in the form of hitting, belting, punching, shoving, flicking, poking, etc. Yelling or sending the child outside or to their room, preferably with a clear explanation of what the problem is, is less harmful to the child's self-esteem than the more violent responses.

'Normal' child development trajectories need to be understood by all parents. Babies and infants have minimal capacities to 'learn' from a smack and virtually no capacity to learn from an explanation. When the child becomes older, verbal explanations need to involve short words, short explanations and simple concepts. If a parent explains things in a way that is outside the cognitive grasp of a child at a specific age, then that way of 'teaching' is a frustration to parents and impossible for the child. As a general principle, parents should be aware that hitting is not an acceptable mode of discipline. Most parents will smack a child sometimes, and that may be accepted as normal in our society. Parents as role models need to develop disciplinary skills that are fair and comprehensible. Such skills allow the child to develop methods of broaching broader social rules and regulations.

Both genders need to be raised with a parental awareness of their similar emotional needs and the need to develop similar basic skills.

Ronald Conway, a clinical psychologist, has seen in therapy a multitude of Australian adult male clients with low self-esteem. He has given considerable thought to this issue. 'It must be accepted by men (particularly fathers) that there is no essential difference in the emotional needs of boys and girls up to the age of puberty, and even far beyond it.'[17] Conway particularly argues against preparing boys for constant 'doing' and 'striving' at the expense of introspection and socialising. Both boys and girls need to play sports for pleasure rather than as competition, spend time alone and just chat with their friends. Both boys and girls need to recognise their feelings and express them in an acceptable way. And both genders need to be able to communicate with other people in a self-expressive and effective manner.

Children of both genders need to have the opportunity to experience dependence as youngsters, independence as teenagers and inter-dependence as mature adults. Young boys should be allowed to be emotionally dependent on their parents for as long as they need to be (young girls usually are). Adolescent and post-adolescent girls should be prepared for the exigencies associated with standing on their own two feet. Adolescent and post-adolescent boys and girls should be prepared to be independent when they wish and inter-dependent if and when they are able. Forced emotional dependence is like raising children to stand on one leg so that if they want to walk they have to have somebody else help them.

Nurturant and expressive skills in boys should be encouraged as much as they are in girls. Technical and instrumental skills in girls should be encouraged as much as they are in boys. Both boys and girls need to develop their bodies by using them in physical activities. Neither boys nor girls should have to associate gymnastics, athletics or sport with having to be the best. If children wish to compete that is fine, but parents, schoolteachers and coaches do not have the right to push talented or vulnerable children into extreme competitiveness, often for their own gains rather than the children's.

SOCIAL POLICY IMPLICATIONS DERIVING FROM MALE GENDER
CONSTRUCTION

*Teenage boys and young men in particular need to discuss their
fears about what they might lose with genuine gender equality
and what they might gain. They should be given opportunities to
discuss these issues in high school and tertiary education settings
with an appropriate male facilitator.*

Who benefits from the present-day public–private split, gendered jobs in the workplace and gendered jobs at home? Is it
every man? I say no. The bourgeoisie have benefited, and in
particular a small percentage of upper middle class and upper
class men. They have accrued the benefits of class, status, wealth
and power. The bulk of men including those in the middle classes
do not experience many of these privileges. Many males in our
society have been lead to believe that they will be upwardly
mobile, rich and powerful; but they are not and the majority will
never be. Males have got less to lose from sexual equality than
they think they have!

Instead of being seduced by false expectations of privilege,
status and wealth, they could anticipate a more comfortable life
in which they are in charge of improving the quality of their
sexual relationships, their emotional relationships and their
parenting relationships. They could gain affection and a feeling of
worthiness from their intimates instead of striving for signs of
superiority and material possessions. To care for others, to care
for themselves and to be cared for because of their personal
attributes rather than their income, car or presents can be a
tremendous gain.

Violent men cling desperately to the need to appear superior.
Looking at gains and losses and discussing them with others may
put patriarchy as it is experienced into a more realistic perspective. Such discussions could be most useful for young men starting
out on sexual relationships. [18] Men who value themselves intrinsically will be less likely to let themselves and others down and less
likely to feel they have failed and respond violently.

*Media gender stereotypes for both women and men need to be
changed over time, and the number of men who behave violently
towards women on screen should be reduced. Legislation could
be neccessary if media owners are intransigent on this issue.*

The argument that men being portrayed as violent on television
has no association with men behaving violently on a day-to-day

basis is fallacious. [19] Boys and men cannot watch hours of television, every week, portraying somebody of their gender being violent in a multiplicity of ways, without it having some meaning for them.

Who gains from this media inundation of images of male violence? I cannot see that the men or women who watch it do. The only winners I can come up with are the producers, directors, television channels and some actors who earn their income from making and purveying these 'entertainments'.

The prevalance of women portrayed as sex objects for commercial advertising and as part of the storyline in movies indicates a fear of women as whole people on the part of television and movie scriptwriters at least. Objectified and commodified females convey strong negative messages about women's worth. 'The objectification of female sexuality which is implied in this form of exchange exposes women to the risk of rape. If something may be bought and sold, it can also be stolen: what can be given can also be taken by force.'[20]

Men are not nearly as violent in their daily lives as they are portrayed to be on television. Let us see movies and read newspaper stories about men being communicative, caring and complex. Let us see movies and read stories about women being productive, innovative and caring. The present images glorify male violence in general and male violence against women in particular. Ordinary men and women gain nothing from this.

POLICY IMPLICATIONS DERIVING FROM PRESENT DAY MALE PERSONAL ATTRIBUTES ARISING FROM GENDER CONSTRUCTION AND REPRODUCTION

Male and female children should be raised with the primary aim of imbuing them with an adequate sense of self-esteem.

A sense of positive self-esteem is the most important characteristic that parents can facilitate for their children. Adults with adequate self-esteem will not need to be violent, and adults with adequate self-esteem will not accept violent treatment. The best aspect of aiming to raise children with positive self-esteem is that it *is* possible and it does not require lots of money.[21] Parents can fail to make their children geniuses, sporting stars, musicians, doctors or moneymakers, but if they understand the principles which allow parents to convey a sense of self-esteem, success is straight forward. The main principles have already been delineated in the section on parent education: they are that children need to be loved unconditionally, they need to be taught that unacceptable behaviour is unequivocally unacceptable and that a child's negative behaviour is not the total child. Hence a child who is 'naughty' is still lovable and a child who excels is praised above and beyond unconditional parental affection.

The genesis of self-esteem is the love that both parents convey to that child because she/he is herself/himself.[22] One of the reasons children are being raised with a lack of self-esteem is that parents who have little self-esteem are limited in their ability to give others affection. If self-esteem is shaky, people often feel that if anybody else feels good about themselves this diminishes their self worth. This may well be one of the paradigms which under-lies wife battering; a male with low self-esteem may perceive his wife as having 'more' (which detracts from his self-esteem in his view) and a battering decreases her self-esteem and is perceived by him to increase his own, ever so briefly. Likewise for rapists. Rape 'is more than a sexual crime, more than simple physical assault: it is an attack on her mind as well as her body, an attack on her whole person undermining her will and self-esteem'.[23]

Unconditional love, which is the seed of self-esteem in children, must not be equated with over-indulgence, laissez-faire parenting or lack of discipline. Children of both genders need emotional and physical expressions of affection. Children of both genders need to be raised with a sense of responsibility for themselves and for others. Boys and girls can become equally competent, caring and responsible adults.

Fathers and mothers are significant gender models for their children.

As Paul Amato's Australian study has shown, children know that fathers are important, but it is not clear to me that fathers actually know that they have a valuable child raising role. Fathers can benefit from knowing that they are needed by their children, and children will benefit from paternal involvement. This is a significant suggestion in that the involvement of fathers in active parenting can break the deprivation cycle involved in male posi-tional identification which sets males up for low self-esteem and gender insecurity. These factors contribute heavily to making a violent male out of an insecure young adult.

Mothers are valuable parents to children. Some mothers know this, perhaps increasingly some mothers feel less sure about their significant role. Even when we have a publicly funded comprehensive child care system with well-paid, well-trained male and female employees who want to love children, teach them skills, and want to allow them to have fun and encourage personal responsibility, parents will continue to have primary child raising responsibilities. Thus *mothers and fathers are needed and are valuable*. Our society needs to convey this message more clearly to us all. Fathers have designated themselves 'as paid employees' and fathers have designated themselves as non child carers. They need to recognise their losses, those of their children and of their wives and reclaim a place as active, caring parents. Mothers can be proud of the important work they have always done and reclaim social value for mothering as well as fathering.

In this chapter I have outlined twenty important changes which need to be made so that we can become a society in which male violence towards females is nonexistent. No doubt these propositions are idiosyncratic and some factors have been overlooked. Oddly, Murray Straus (1977) came up with 21 policy implications deriving from six social–structural causal factors. Many of the conclusions I draw are similar to his.[24]

The main difference between his suggestions and mine is that I see male personal characteristics as *the* factors within a particular social structure which ultimately are sufficient for any man to become a batterer. This is not psychological reductionism. It is social realism. The causal clusters which Straus considers impinge on all men. From his analysis I draw the conclusion that all men (with a few upper middle class and upper class exemptions of course) are battering their wives. They are not. It is the low self-esteem and the high dependence which are sufficient for a man to behave violently towards a woman in the *last* instance. It is the *social structural factors* which set the men up for the possibility of violence in the *first* instance. Those factors must be dealt with first if we are to prevent male violence rather than pick up the female pieces.

6 | Conclusions

The purpose of this chapter is to articulate and review key concepts and arguments. This work has drawn out concepts and processes from macro-social, interpersonal and intra-psychic theories in an attempt to offer a comprehensive explanation of the construction and reproduction of violent males in our society. In the process I have rendered these men who are violent towards women somewhat more visible than they usually are. Needless to say I have not provided *the* answer to this question but I have offered some answers. In the first chapter I investigate partriarchy and its interaction with capitalism. My working definition of patriarchy is that of gendered power relations which by-and-large confer material, social, sexual and ideological advantages to males. Patriarchy manifests itself differently in various societies and classes and in different historical periods.

PATRIARCHAL POWER RELATIONS

I begin with Deborah McIntyre's premises.

> Fundamental, then, to the understanding of wife beating...is an analysis of the functioning of patriarchal society and its contemporary mediation via the nuclear family...In so far as the patterns of relating engendered [in the marital relationship] can be described as involving dominance and submission, then wife beating can be seen as falling at one end of a continuum, the end at which dominance is given an explicit, and violent, form. As such, it constitutes an overt restatement of the actuality of patriarchal power.[1]

The patriarchal public–domestic division as it is manifested in our society makes two major contributions towards the possibility of male violence against females. Firstly the division separates women from men in both the public and the private domains. In the public arena this provides males with multiple situations for male mutual support and camaraderie. Secondly in both the public and private domains the structures hinder female mutual support and camaraderie. Both of these factors, given the patriarchal underpinnings of our society, increase the likelihood of male unity and female disunity which exacerbate tendencies for male vio-

118

lence and inhibit tendencies for female support for female victims. Given that most male violence towards females takes place in the domestic domain, this also contributes to the hidden nature of such violence and the invisibility of the perpetrators.

> It is the man who can occupy the interface between groups. It is men who discover novel people and goods, renew old acquaintances and control many of the networks of communication...Occupying the interface, males also have access to the different and innovative, again another source of power.[2]

In the public domain, with its patriarchal infrastructures, men wield economic, political, social and ideological power. Amongst many other social norms, men directly and indirectly determine the levels of violence that are acceptable at macro- and micro-social levels. Thus men determine the legitimacy of international and intra-national wars, police practices, rape and wife battering, to name a few. Some writers such as David Gil deem our society to have high levels of intrinsic violence.[3] Cross-cultural researchers have found that wife batterers are more common in societies in which women's status is inferior to that of men's and in societies in which 'brutality and cruelty' are prevalent.[4]

The practices of the labour market, welfare and tax systems place women in our society in a materially inferior position. Women's rates of pay are lower and their opportunities for promotion are fewer than men's. Married women who consider themselves 'unemployed' cannot claim the unemployment benefit in their own right if their husband is working full time as the unit which is means tested by the Department of Social Security is the couple's income. Even though such a woman cannot legitimately receive the benefit for her own purposes, her husband can claim her dependence by virtue of her 'unemployment' in the form of the dependent spouse tax rebate. Thus ideologies and practices built into the labour market-welfare-tax consortium are patriarchal by nature and impede women's economic independence.

The study of a nationally (United States) representative sample of 2143 men and women by Debra Kalmuss and Murray Straus investigated the relationship between wives' dependency on marriage and battering.

> The independent variables were indexes of wives' objective (economic) and subjective (perceived) marital dependency...both dimensions of dependency were positively related to abuse...These results indicate that it is economic and not psychological dependency which keeps women in severely abusive marriages.[5]

Male gender stereotypes have emanated from patriarchal practices and beliefs. Marc Fasteau has outlined four assumptions which shape men's views of women and *ipso facto* of men.

First, we—men and women both—believe in the either/or theory of human personality...Second, men believe that to be masculine they have to be radically different from women. Third, men believe they are better than women and that...they must dominate and outperform them. Fourth, the areas assigned to women are thought of as less important and difficult than those assigned to men, and men, to keep their masculine identification and status, try to stay out of them.[6]

Thus male and female stereotypes are polarised and the male-designated 'inferior' qualities are assigned to the female and the 'superior' characteristics are attributed to males. It is therefore males who have determined that men are enterprising, logical, tough, powerful, aggressive, decisive, dominant, self-reliant, stern and arrogant.[7] And it is from these stereotypes that we learn that males are allowed, if not encouraged, to be violent.

THE MODERN FAMILY

In chapter 2 I narrow my focus to marriage and the family. Diana Gittins emphasises the patriarchal meanings attached to the notion of family in our society.

Imbued in western patriarchal ideology...are a number of important and culturally specific beliefs about sexuality, reproduction, parenting and the power relationships between age groups and between the sexes. The sum total of these beliefs make up a strong *symbol-system which is labelled as the family.*[8]

The family embodies these ideologies and practices which derive from patriarchal gendered power relations. Her definition of the family leans too heavily in the ideological direction, but Mark Poster emphasises practices. 'In the modern family, new forms of the oppression of children and women arose which were dependent upon critical mechanisms of authority and love, of intense ambivalent emotions'.[9] Power relations, gender relations and emotional intensity are thus built into the family and the marital relationship as we know them.

The simplest articulation of the fact that the family is built on a gendered power base is the belief in, and the practice of, the man as 'head of the family'. If this maxim is taken seriously, and there is no reason to disregard it[10], the family is potentially a major site for the exercise of male power. This power will not be absolute, it will be contested, but for the man who believes in his entitlement to such a position, it may be the bottom line. The family is therefore a site of conflict. According to Letha and John Scanzoni, there are four ways of dealing with conflict: escape; submission; righting the balance; or violence. It is difficult to escape the family; submission may contribute towards a resentment log; and righting the balance requires skills in negotiating, bargaining and co-operation.[11] Dichotomised genders and the complementary interactions deriving from them, both of which devolve on patriarchal power relations, are not conducive to the mutual respect, communication skills and assertiveness needed to right the balance. Hence marital conflict may lead to the fourth option of violence.

The family is a powered site and a site of conflict. Proportionally more men expect to be head of the family than women expect them to be. Thus many men are in the position of living cognitive, affective and practical contradictions. They expect to be boss, but the anticipated levels of amicable deference are not forthcoming. They have believed the 'promise' of masculinity, but in reality they do not get to comfortably wield power in either the work place or the home.

These contradictions of male experience may exacerbate the patriarchal tendencies to separate male from female. As the family is inherently conflictual, males may avoid testing out the realities of the extent of their power by staying away from home. Hence the attraction of work and the pub. Work does not only provide an 'escape' from the family, but it offers males a positive and appropriate place of their own. Marc Fasteau considers the workplace to be a significant male domain.

> The masculine ethos recognizes the importance of work. In fact, work is the area of life into which 'masculine' traits are thought to fit best and the principal adult arena for proving one's masculinity. Our dominant social philosophy, influenced by and influencing the masculine stereotype, makes work an essential determinant of moral worth.[13]

Hence the significance of gendered places at work. 'The reorganization of the labour process in ways that perpetuate...gender divisions at work, similarly reflect protectionist strategies which allow for some assertion of masculine power'.[14] Within the family, work is also frequently gendered; some jobs are 'hers', others 'his', the important issue being the separation of the tasks rather than the content of the activities.

The job within the family which is most obviously gendered is that of parenting, so much so that parenting is often understood as being synonymous with mothering. Mothering fits into

Fasteau's fourth assumption—that parenting is women's work, it is 'easy', and men to emphasise their masculinity should stay out of it.

> Panegyrics to mother love abound in the professional as well as the popular literature. It is supposed to have unique, totally selfless, all-forgiving qualities which make it irreplaceable...the uncritical zeal with which men seize on this argument suggests strongly that it masks other sources of resistance.[15]

Such appeals to myth, idealisation and fantasy are sure signs that something else is going on here.

Men have relegated women to the work of child raising on the grounds that women bear babies therefore they should raise them, that it is 'natural' for women to do so and only the biological mother can do it best. One pragmatic reason for people to delegate tasks, devalue them and rationalise the inevitability of it all is that they cannot do the job themselves, apart from whether they wish to or not. Men have not been prepared for parenting.

> For individual fathers, apart from the amount of time spent on job or career, the most serious obstacle to developing rewarding and useful relationships with their children is an inflexibly masculine personality. Small children cannot be dealt with on the basis of reason alone...One has to confront and deal with their feelings. But to understand and accept another person's feelings one must be able to put oneself in his or her place, to experience a little of the feeling oneself. For men who are uncomfortable with and repress their own emotions, especially weak, dependent, 'childlike' emotions, this is difficult.[16]

Generations of males who have been taught to eschew parenting responsibilities have produced men with minimal skills in these areas.

The unequal division of labour with regard to child care in our society has many significant sequelae. Mothers forgo income on the birth of their children and they become more economically and emotionally dependent on their husbands—the latter being due to the social isolation which invariably accompanies the role of child raiser in our society. Fathers thus wield considerable material and emotional power over mothers and children. This is the site in which the promises of masculinity are almost redeemed. Male violence in this setting under these structural conditions may be seen as an extension of 'normal' male material and emotional power advantage. If violence is perpetrated, it is these very powered relations which mediate heavily against the practical possibilities of women and children escaping. And it is these powered relations which have rendered much violence against women invisible, and allowed violent men themselves to remain invisible as such. Sexual practices of course are also hidden within 'the family'.

In chapter 3 I proceed further into the family to examine how masculinity is constructed within this domain. It is within the family in the first instance that the promise of masculinity is perceived by the boy, and parents live out their power differentials. Wini Breines and Linda Gordon highlight the connections between being male and being violent.

> ...all violence must be seen in the context of wider power relations; violence is not necessarily deviant or fundamentally different from other means of exerting power over another person. Thus, violence cannot be accurately viewed as a set of isolated events but must be placed in an entire social context...There are patterns to violence between intimates which only an analysis of gender, and its centrality to the family, can illuminate.[17]

The family is also the location in which expressions and behaviours associated with intimacy are experienced, observed and learned first of all. It is here that nascent perceptions of sex, sexuality and sexual practices are garnered.

Breines and Gordon demand an analysis of gender at the unconscious as well as conscious levels.

> No act of violence is simply the pitting of one individual against another; each contains deep cultural and psychological meanings. At the same time, no act of violence is merely the expression of a social problem (or a culture) such as poverty or unemployment or male dominance; each is also the personal act of a unique individual... How male supremacy, class and race domination, and acute social stress inform specific acts of violence requires an analysis of psychic processes.[18]

Hence we cannot remain at macro-social or surface levels of explication alone.

What needs to be done first is to bridge the macro-social and the individual. Second, the conscious and unconscious processes within the batterer must be uncovered. Here I make use of Nancy Chodorow's pivotal concept of positional identification. Positional identification provides these two bridges and answers the

following question. How do laughable male stereotypical characteristics become so much a part of the inner life of a man that he
will beat his wife to defend them in himself?

Positional identification is a way of learning to become 'oneself'
and a way of learning to be male. The crucial aspect of positional
identification for these purposes is the expurgation of emotional
experience from the learning processes. The boy cannot be loved
by Inspector Gadget, say, nor can he love Inspector Gadget—the
medium precludes this. Although the boy can recognise at his
level of cognitive development male characteristics and can emu-
late requisite behaviour and repeat apposite phrases, there will be
no emotional reward coming from the television. Thus the boy is
still emotionally 'deprived'. This lack of emotional reward may be
built into his learning repertoire as the cognitive—affective split.
Emotions are not part of learning and learning is not an emotional experience. Thinking is not informed by feeling and feeling is
not informed by thinking. This is particularly so for the violent
male. Violent men are internally overwhelmed by emotions that
have lost their attachment to the original source: out-of-control
feelings are acted out without cognitive countermands.

As the positionally identified boy looks beyond his family for
indicators of masculinity, he also realises that 'male' is that which
is not 'female'. Thus masculinity gains a negative definition, one
that in actuality may be more achievable than other definitions.
Here his primary affective identification with his mother is at least
unconsciously an impediment. To counter that early symbiosis,
the young boy's sense of self narrows so that emotionally charged
identifications with the mother are dissociated. To find himself,
he unconsciously narrows down his sense of self and erects a
metaphorical brick wall in defence. Thus we have the narrow and
rigid male ego boundaries.

There are two significant consequences arising out of narrow
ego boundaries. The first is that intimacy and/or sexuality may
reactivate repressed emotions pertaining to infantile symbiosis
with the mother. Emotional closeness or sexual activity with a
female may evoke intense ambivalence—the desire for intimacy
and fear of intimacy.[19] The second sequel is that the narrowed
sense of self results in a narrowed sense of responsibility. This
manifests as an underdeveloped propensity to experience appropriate guilt, conscious and unconscious denial of appropriate
responsibility for one's own actions and the possibility of unconscious projection of responsibility onto another. The violent male
bears all of these signs: he is hostile-dependent; does not expe-

rience appropriate guilt; denies responsibility; and projects blame for his actions onto his partner.

No matter what is being said within the family, being done out in the street or performed on television, children of both genders take in power relations. They recognise the way these are lived, what the patterns are, who are the winners and losers and how the protocols work. This is high-powered experiential learning within the family. Such learning may never be discussed and the processes that the child observes and absorbs may never even be named or articulated by the child. This is the power of early intense learning which takes place in the family and is one of the keys to the intergenerational transmission of gendered power relations—patriarchy. Boys, whether positionally identified or not, learn that parents wield profound power over children, and that men, in general and in particular, wield much more power over women than vice versa. Thus power-wielding is a signpost of masculinity in our society.

VIOLENCE—LOW SELF-ESTEEM—HIGH EMOTIONAL DEPENDENCY NEXUS

Norman Denzin recognise the connections between wielding power, poor self-esteem and violence.

> As he attempts to impose his will on the subjectivity of his spouse or his child the violent subject annihilates the other's consciousness and being in the world...He has the flesh of the other in his grip, while the other's will and freedom slips from his grasp...What he attempts to regain through violent means (including the loss of or threat to self-esteem, the loss of self-control and control over the other) is destroyed through his violent actions.[20]

In chapter 4 I discuss two male characteristics which, in combination, make the difference between the 'normal' male I have discerned in the previous chapters and the violent male. These are low self-esteem and high emotional dependency, both of which derive from male positional identification. The low self-esteem emerges from the lack of positive affective feedback to the male infant/boy and/or the presence of negative affective feedback from the father. The high emotional dependency derives in the first instance from the modern family's emotional intensity and small size.

By focusing on low self-esteem at the extreme end of one male continuum and high emotional dependency on another male continuum, I am emphasising the significance of the emotional domain in human life. Theories which do not give our inner experiences their due power will never fully explain male violence towards intimates.

> *Violence will be defined here as the attempt to regain, through the use of emotional and physical force, something that has been lost.* What has been lost is directly traceable to the self of the violent person. The self and its feelings are at the core of violent conduct. If emotionality is understood as self-feelings directed towards self and others, violence can be understood only from the point of view of feeling, self-reflective, violent individuals.[21]

Denzin is one of few theorists who is able to acknowledge and highlight the emotional underpinnings of male violence towards females.

The main constituent of self-esteem is how one feels about oneself. Thus it is not a rational phenomenon and it cannot be significantly altered by short-term behavioural interventions. The affective ingredients go back to early childhood, which explains the continuity of self-esteem levels. Boys who develop low self-esteem are likely to feel insecure about their sexuality as the two are closely related, especially in males in our society.[22] 'All [male] children who have been in doubt about their sexual role exaggerate the traits which they consider masculine'.[23] I would go further and say that men with low self-esteem and gender insecurity (conscious or unconscious) will endeavour to make social compensations for their inner affective discomfort. There are stereotypical arenas in which men may enhance their sense of being male: sport, work, alcohol consumption and the wielding of power over women. Needless to say this compendium is not exhaustive.

Excelling in sport is curtailed by age, time, income and motivation. Thus many men will not be able to easily compensate for their personal feelings of insecurity in the domain of sport. Being successful at work is constrained by such things as class, education, talent, opportunity, experience, social skills and economic climate. Even though many men will be able to shore up their view of themselves in the paid work environment, others will not be able to do so. Drinking alcohol is more readily achievable in that no skills are required, and it is cheap enough so that only the unemployed and very heavy drinkers will be impeded by costs. Wielding power over women is even less expensive, requires minimal skills (given macro-social support) and can take place in the privacy of the home in 'sure winner' situations.

For practical purposes, the male with low self-esteem who feels the need to achieve these positive 'ideals' is likely to fail unless he comes from the upper middle class. This leaves the more negative 'ideals' for the bulk of working class and middle class men. Hence the popularity of drinking alcohol and wielding of power within the family—often a dangerous combination with violent men. This argument supports the notion that men who cannot 'succeed' in the public domain or have few 'resources' will resort to alcohol and/or violence. It is not that such men actively choose those paths: they are affectively (and sometimes unconsciously) propelled towards alcohol and/or violence to anaesthetise or compensate for their feelings of insecurity.

The final question that needs to be asked to distinguish batterers, incest perpetrators and partner rapists[24] from other violent males is why the violence is directed towards an intimate. Here we face the significance of males with high emotional dependency needs and the patriarchal construction of male sexuality. The highly emotionally dependent males are those who were positionally identified and received insufficient unconditional nurturance from their primary care givers. Such males remain emotionally needy. Emotionally dependent people cannot stand on their own two (affective) feet. They do not feel that they are real, whole or alive unless they receive continuous nurturance or deference from another/others. A spouse-like partner is thus ideal.

Male sexuality in our society continues to be strongly anti auto-erotic and strongly homophobic. Hence males are raised to be sexually active-aggressive and there are powerful proscriptions against masturbation and/or homosexual practices as socially acceptable long-term sexual practices. Males socialised to be 'sexual' are left with females as the most obvious targets for male sexual gratification. Again a spouse-like partner seems ideal. It is modern family practices and male gender and sexuality construction in our society that makes some males primarily violent towards females with whom they have an intimate relationship.

Thus far I have summarised my thesis—that is, the factors that contribute to the construction of violent men in our society. What I have presented is an 'ideal' type theory which consists of generalisations and abstractions which may be contradicted by some sub-groups evidence. The construction of violent males is not simple, but it is possible to discern a range of social practices that make significant contributions to these processes. My thesis rests on three particular continua. There is the personal-positional identification continuum which, at the latter end, produces males who are highly likely to have characteristics which are prerequisites of the capacity to violate females. The second is the high-low self-esteem continuum. The third is the emotional independence-interdependence-dependence continuum.

It is impossible to say what extent of male positional identification will produce a man with low enough self-esteem and high enough emotional dependence to be violent towards females. However I do make the general statement: the raising of boys in the positionally identified mode (in our society) will produce men with low self-esteem and high emotional dependency needs who are likely to be violent towards their women intimates. The greater the father distance (especially emotional), the lower the male self-esteem and the higher the emotional dependence. Hence the more positional the male identification processes, the more unsure he will be of his masculinity and his sexuality and the more likely he will attack women sexually and/or violently.

THEORETICAL LEVELS AND SOCIOLOGICAL THEORISTS

As the social construction of the violent male arises out of complex processes and interactions, so in this book I deal with a range of levels of social theory. The work spans macro-social, micro-social and intrapsychic theories and their interfaces. Patriarchal and capitalist power relations interpenetrate each other at the macro-social level. Within this theoretical domain lie such concepts as class; gender stereotypes; the state; public-private divisions; the labour-welfare-tax nexus; marriage; family; mothering; fathering.

Bob Connell's *Gender and Power* (which I read after I had written the bulk of this thesis) starts in this domain. I began this book with a chapter on patriarchy because I believe that patriarchy-capitalism provides the foundations which ultimately underpin other theoretical levels. Connell's demand for a theory of social structure is of the same order.

> ...the concept of structure is more than another term for 'pattern' and refers to the intractability of the social world. It reflects the experience of being up against something, of limits on freedom; and also the experience of being able to operate by proxy, to produce results one's own capacities would not allow. The concept of *social* structure expresses the constraints that lie in a given form of social organisation (rather than, say, physical facts about the world).[25]

Thus Connell begins in the macro-domain as does Mark Poster, Nancy Chodorow and this work. In pursuit of gender, the family, mothering and the batterer respectively, each of us has been compelled to bridge the macro- and intra-psychic levels of theory. This macro–micro link is in itself a major concern for some contemporary sociologists.[26]

Poster demands theoretical analyses at the psychological level, everyday life and the interface of family and society. Like Connell, he emphasises power. Although history is significant for Poster, he does not concentrate so much on the structured nature of labour. However he is very concerned with emotion and how macro-structures, mediated by the family, have changed the nature and intensity of emotional life over time. Poster emphasises the coincidence of power and affect in parental relations with children within the modern family.

> ... the basic structural features of the bourgeois family persist: the child is confronted by two adults from whom it must obtain satisfaction for all its needs for love and nurturance. In this context, the child must learn to love people who appear far more powerful than it. Sexual stereotyping and internalized authority are built firmly into this family structure.[27]

Chodorow, rather more like Connell, begins with capitalism and patriarchy.

> The distinction that we easily draw however, between the economy ('men's world') and the family ('women's world'), and the analytic usefulness in our separation of the mode of production and the sex-gender system, does not mean that these two systems are not empirically or structurally connected. Rather, they are linked (and almost inextricably intertwined).[28]

Like Poster, she also recognises the significance of the emotional concentration in the modern parent (mother)—child relationship. Chodorow's work is at the same interface as the other two theorists but she focuses on labour and object-choice at the expense of power. More than the other authors I have drawn from, Chodorow highlights the unconscious and the dynamic relationships between the intrapsychic and macro-social levels.

> I focus primarily on the ways that family structure and process, in particular the asymmetrical organisation of parenting, effect unconscious psychic structure and process... All aspects of psychic structure, character, and emotional and erotic life are social, constituted through a 'history of object-choices'. This history, dependent on the individual personalities and behaviour of those who happen to interact with a child, is also socially patterned according to the family structure and prevalent psychological modes of a society.[29]

THIS THEORY AND BEYOND

In the final chapter, I consider the practical question: what can be done to eradicate male violence towards females from our society? A lot has to be done on many fronts because of the complexity of the processes, and their intransigence, in that we are involved in such domains as the intergenerational transmission of culture and the unconscious. Changes can be made—as they are, one way or another, always. The steps that I outline are very similar to those made by others before me.[30]

Patriarchal power is not a monolithic and homogenous thing that we can dismantle simply. It is a complex series of interconnected structures, practices and beliefs, and these powered fields need to be recognised, resisted and changed. The only way we can bring about such changes is by many people challenging the status quo, doing things differently and questioning values and beliefs. I have emphasised about twenty major strategies that I consider to be significant in the last chapter. An underlying theme of this book is making male violence visible especially to men, and dragging the perpetrators out into the open to render them and their actions visible.

Now I need to look back over this whole work and discuss what I have done above and beyond explicating a theory which reveals some of the specific ways our society constructs violent males. One of the obvious things I have done is contribute to the body of Australian literature on wife battering. Out of about 160 articles or books I have found on this topic, only 10 per cent have been written by Australians; and the majority of references these writers have cited are from the United Kingdom or the United States of America. Internationally, there is a dearth of research on batterers. In Australia, so far as I am aware of published literature, only Frances Baum *et al*, Suzanne Hatty and David Wehner have tackled the batterer himself.[31] I add this document to this very small body of local knowledge and research.

As Clare Burton states in the introduction to her book *Subordination*, 'the most significant omission in this book is a discussion of Chodorow's work'.[32] This is an omission in gender studies in Australia that has not been fully rectified even though Connell briefly discusses major points from Nancy Chodorow and Dorothy Dinnerstein in *Gender and Power*[33]. My chapter on male gender construction is built on Chodorow's work on female gender construction. Chodorow is writing about the construction of femininity consciously and unconsciously in the context of our gendered division of labour. My work in a small way elaborates on some of her crucial concepts and processes. Chodorow is concerned with the 'normal' production and reproduction of motherhood and femininity in our society. I have utilised insights from her work to explain the 'normal' production and reproduction of masculinity and the production of the violent male. The two are not entirely separable. Thus I have extended Chodorow's theory of gender construction and applied it in my search for the connections between masculinity and violence in our society.

Chris Weedon rightly points out: 'the difference that Chodorow posits between 'real' personal and positional identification is *the definitive* factor in her account of the differential constitution of femininity and masculinity'.[34] I take this observation a step further and make the claim that male positional identification, which clearly arises from the gendered divisions of labour inside and outside the family, is the definitive factor that sets up some proportion of males in our society with specific characteristics which encourage them to resort to violence. Positional identification has become an important theoretical tool for me. It provides a necessary bridge between the unconscious and the conscious, the unconscious being notoriously inaccessible to sociologists.

One of the sequelae of male positional identification is the cognitive-affective split. The second major consequence of male positional identification that writers (for example, Connell, Weedon) mention but do not elaborate on, is the narrow and rigid male ego boundary. I push this concept even further and relate the narrow male ego boundary to the overuse of such unconscious defense mechanisms as denial and projection. There is plenty of evidence in the clinical literature to show that violent men resort over-much to such defenses. Practically, this means that positionally identified males take insufficient responsibility for their own actions and inactions. This is clearly related to superego phenomena as well. Here I disagree with writers such as Chodorow and Connell who concur with Freud that males in our society develop a 'strong superego'.[35] Because the positionally identified male's affective ties with his father are not strong, the internationalisation of the father's superego as his own (Freud) is not as strong. In personally identified females (the majority), the affective ties with the mother are strong, the cognitive-affective ties with the mother are strong, the cognitive-affective split is nonexistent and the identification with the morality of the previous generation is stronger. Thus women tend to experience overresponsibility and excess guilt (Chodorow); and positionally identified men experience underresponsibility and insufficiently developed guilt which manifest as denial and projection.

Overall, I have drawn from Chodorow's work and elaborated on a number of the concepts she utilises. In the process of attempting to explain the construction of men who are violent towards women intimates in our society, I believe I have contributed towards the possibility of a systematic social theory of gender. Finally, the work analyses and integrates structures and processes from macro-social, micro-social and intrapsychic levels of society.

For myself, this work has at least partially explained how our society produces and reproduces masculine insecurities, misogyny and male violence against females. I hope that this book renders perpetrators of violence against women more visible. It is not acceptable that such men can hide with the assistance of the patriarchal premises embedded in the law, police practices, pub conversations and middle class avoidance and denial. If our society is going to work against such violences, men collectively must acknowledge male violence and start to take responsibility for themselves, their actions and their beliefs. If our society is going to act against such violences, we must deal assertively with the perpetrators and offer them opportunities to change themselves. Such programmes need to be instigated by men who are well aware of their own sexist and violent tendencies and who can facilitate group processes that are profoundly challenging on the one hand and supportive on the other. Some violent men are not motivated to change themselves, and these men must be appropriately and consistently dealt with by the police and the law and jailed for their crimes.

Notes

Introduction

1 Snell *et al* (1964), Faulk (1974) and Scott (1974) discussed in J. Renvoize *Web of Violence* Harmondsworth, 1979, p. 44, p. 45 and p. 53 respectively

2 Renvoize *Web of Violence* pp. 41–63

3 *ibid.* pp. 192–9. Arnon Bentovim's victim-blaming is considerably watered down now and is replaced by apparent approval of certain sorts of incest. See A. Bentovim *et al Child Sexual Abuse within the Family* London: Wright, 1989, p. 17 and p. 33

4 N. Shainess *Sweet Suffering. Woman as Victim* Indianapolis: Bobbs-Merrill, 1984, pp. 125–55

5 J. Deschner *The Hitting Habit* New York: Macmillan, 1984, pp. 13–22

6 Renvoize *Web of Violence* pp. 53–64

7 *ibid.* p. 196

8 Deschner *The Hitting Habit* pp. 41–5

9 Shainess *Sweet Suffering* pp. 143–9

10 Renvoize *Web of Violence* pp. 194–8

11 *ibid.* p. 10

12 Deschner *The Hitting Habit* p. 14

13 *ibid.* p. 46–9

14 See H. Kaplan and B. Sadock *Modern Synopsis of Comprehensive Textbook of Psychiatry* Baltimore: Williams & Williams, 1985. Personality disorders in general, pp. 361–5, antisocial personality disorders, pp. 372–5

15 E. Gondolf *Men Who Batter: An Integrated Approach for Stopping Wife Abuse* Holmes Beach: Learning Publications, 1985; D. Sonkin, D. Martin and L. Walker *The Male Batterer. A Treatment Approach* New York: Springer, 1985

16 Some male writers have, of course, made a start. See H. Brod (ed.) *The Making of Masculinities* Boston: Allen & Unwin, 1987; R. Connell *Gender & Power* Sydney: Allen & Unwin, 1987; M. Fasteau *The Male Machine* New York: Delta, 1975; H. Goldberg *The Hazards of Being Male* New York: Signet, 1976; S. Jourard *The Transparent Self* New York: Van Nostrand, 1971; A. Metcalf and M. Humphries (eds) *The Sexuality of Men* London: Pluto Press, 1985; J. Pleck *The Myth of Masculinity* Cambridge: Massachusetts Institute of Technology Press, 1981

17 Richard Gelles and Murray Straus spring to mind most promptly

18 Maria Roy and Suzanne Steinmetz are examples

19 For example R. Gelles and M. Straus 'Determinants of Violence in the Family: Toward a Theoretical Integration' in W. Burr *et al* (eds)

Contemporary Theories About the Family vol. I., New York: Free Press, 1979. See figures 21.2 and 21.3
This 'scientific' mode continues. L. Baron and M. Straus 'Four Theories of Rape' *Social Problems* vol. 34 (5), pp. 467–88. See figures 1 and 2; and tables 1 and 2

20 Office of the Status of Women (1988) *Community Attitudes towards Domestic Violence in Australia* Sydney: Public Policy Research Centre, 1988. Quoted in the *Australian*, 9 March 1988, p. 1

21 The main problem with the thesis that I put up is that it is premised upon a female–male two parent family. I have done this to make it easier to present the theory clearly. I recognise that such a family is only one of a range of possible families. The female single parent family is increasingly becoming predominant. I certainly cannot support the notions that 'any man is better than none' or that 'children need a father' no matter how awful. I support the rights of women to live as they prefer.

1 Patriarchal contributions to male violence towards women

1 R. Dobash and R. Dobash *Violence Against Wives* London: Open Books, 1980, p. 7

2 ibid. p. 10

3 R. McDonough and R. Harrison 'Patriarchy & Relations of Production' in A. Kuhn & A. Wolpe (eds) *Feminism & Materialism* London: Routledge & Kegan Paul, 1978, p. 25

4 C. Pateman *The Sexual Contract* Cambridge: Polity Press, 1988, pp. 30–8

5 R. Connell *Which Way is Up?* Sydney: George Allen & Unwin, 1983, p. 51

6 ibid. p. 56

7 D. Morgan *The Family, Politics & Social Theory* London: Routledge & Kegan Paul, 1985, pp. 224–5

8 M. Stacey and M. Price *Women, Power & Politics* London: Tavistock, 1981, p. 3

9 P. Bachrach and M. Baratz *Power & Poverty. Theory & Practice* New York: Oxford University, 1979, p. 11

10 ibid. p. 24

11 ibid pp. 30–1

12 ibid. p. 33

13 ibid. p. 34

14 K. Millett *Sexual Politics* London: Virago, 1979, p. 58

15 D. Gittins *The Family in Question, Changing Households & Familiar Ideologies*, Basingstoke: Macmillan, 1986, p. 36

16 J. Westergaard and H. Resler quoted in Stacey & Price *Women, Power & Politics* p. 9

17 Z. Eisenstein (ed.) *Capitalism, Patriarchy & the Case for Socialist Feminism* New York: Monthly Review Press, 1979, p. 5

18 ibid. p. 8

19 ibid. p. 17

20 ibid. p. 28

21 E. Zaretsky *Capitalism, The Family & Personal Life* New York: Harper Colophon, 1976, p. 61

22 H. Hartmann 'Capitalism, Patriarchy & Job Segregation by Sex' in Z. Eisenstein *Capitalism, Patriarchy, & The Case for Socialist Feminism*, p. 216

23 ibid. p. 219

24 Z. Eisenstein, p. 50

25 Zaretsky *Capitalism* p. 65

26 ibid. p. 113

27 A male who works with battering men, cited in S. Schechter *Women & Violence* Boston: South End, 1982, p. 221

28 J. Garrett-Gooding and R. Senter 'Attitudes & Acts of Sexual Aggression on a University Campus', *Sociological Inquiry* 57 (4), 1987, p. 366; and G. McCall and N. Shields 'Social & Structural Factors in Family Violence' in M. Lystad (ed.) *Violence in the Home* New York: Brunner/Hazel, 1986, p. 101

29 M. Rosaldo and L. Lamphere (eds) *Woman, Culture & Society* California: Stanford University Press, 1974, p. 23

30 M. Straus 'A Sociological Perspective on the Prevention & Treatment of Wifebeating' in M. Roy (ed.) *Battered Women* New York: Van Nostrand, 1977, p. 200

31 See, for example, C. Clement *Opera, or the Undoing of Women* London: Virago 1989; and P. Conrad *A Song of Love & Death. The Meaning of Opera* London: Hogarth Press, 1987. Both acknowledge male violence against females in opera

32 Straus *Battered Women* p. 200

33 J. Hanmer 'Violence & the Social Control of Women' in G. Littlejohn *et al* (eds) *Power & the State* London: Croom Helm, 1978, p. 219

34 R. Hamilton *The Liberation of Women. A Study of Patriarchy & Capitalism*, London: George Allen & Unwin, 1978, p. 68

35 Straus *Battered Women* p. 197

36 ibid. pp. 215–6

37 J. Scutt *Even in the Best of Homes. Violence in the Family* Ringwood: Penguin, 1983, p. 257

38 M. Cordell 'New Ways to Deal with the Domestic' *Sydney Morning Herald* 13 September 1986:13

39 S. McIllhatton (1984) 'Domestic Violence: Remedies under N.S.W. and Federal Legislation' *Law Society Journal*, August p. 439

40 H. Brod (ed.) *The Making of Masculinities* Boston: Allen & Unwin, 1987, p. 51

41 Quoted in Cordell *Sydney Morning Herald* p. 13

42 See J. Stubbs and A. Wallace 'Protecting Victims of Domestic Violence?' in M. Findlay and R. Hogg (eds) *Understanding Crime & Criminal Justice* Sydney: The Law Book Company, 1988, pp. 62–70

43 D. Bell 'The Police Response to Domestic Violence: An Exploratory Study' *Police Studies*, 7 (1), p. 27. See also S. Hatty 'Woman Battering as a Social Problem' *A & N Z Journal of Sociology* 23 (1), p. 39, and Scutt *Even in the Best of Homes* p. 223

44 J. Scutt 'Domestic Violence the Police Response' in C. O'Donnell and J. Craney (eds) *Family Violence in Australia* Melbourne: Longman Cheshire, 1982, p. 111

45 L. Sherman and R. Berk 'The Specific Deterrent Effects of Arrest for Domestic Assault' *American Sociological Review* vol. 49, 1984, p. 261

46 E. Stark *et al* 'Medicine & Patriarchal Violence: the Social Construction of a "Private Event"' *International Journal of Health Services* 9 (3), 1979, pp. 469–71

47 D. Kurz 'Emergency Department Responses to Battered Women' *Social Problems* 34 (1), 1987, p. 79

48 Scutt *Even in the Best of Homes* p. 227

49 Office of Status of Women *Community Attitudes Towards Domestic Violence in Australia* Sydney: Public Policy Research Centre, 1988, p. 23

50 B. Cass 'Population Policies & Family Policies' in C. Baldock and B. Cass (eds) *Women, Social Welfare & the State* Sydney: George Allen & Unwin, 1983, pp. 181–5

51 H. Land 'Who Cares for the Family?' *Journal of Social Policy* 7 (3), 1978, p. 258

52 Straus *Battered Women* pp. 210–11

53 C. Keens and B. Cass *Fiscal Welfare: Some Aspects of Australian Tax Policy* Sydney: Social Welfare Research Centre, 1982, p. 42

54 M. Edwards 'Social Effects of Taxation' in J. Wilkes (ed.) *The Politics of Taxation* Sydney: Hodder & Stoughton, 1980, p. 143

55 Keens and Cass *Fiscal Welfare* p. 44

56 See H. Land 'Who Cares for the Family?' p. 282; and M. Barrett and M. McIntosh 'The "Family Wage"' in E. Whitelegg *et al* (eds) *The Changing Experience of Women* Oxford: Martin Robertson, 1982, p. 79

57 The *Australian* 3–4 February 1990, 'Equality at Work Remains Elusive', 'Australian Bureau of Statistics' data cited, p. 46

58 R. Gelles 'Violence in the American Family' in D. Martin (ed.) *Violence & the Family* New York: John Wiley, 1978, p. 59

59 D. Martin *Battered Wives* San Francisco: Volcano Press, 1981, p. 83

60 C. Burton *Subordination, Feminism & Social Theory* Sydney: George Allen & Unwin, 1985, p. 105. See also J. Roe 'The End is Where We Start From: Women & Welfare Since 1901' in Baldock and Cass *Women, Social Welfare & The State* pp. 13–14 and E. Wilson *Women & the Welfare State* London: Tavistock, 1977, p. 9

61 M. McIntosh 'The State & the Oppression of Women' in A. Kuhn and A. Wolpe (eds) *Feminism & Materialism* p. 257

62 W. Borrie (chairman National Population Inquiry) *Population and Australia*, volume I, Canberra: Australian Government Publishing Service, 1975, p. 59

63 Information given by telephone from a senior social worker, Department of Social Security, 27 May 1988

64 Roe *Women, Social Welfare & The State* p. 12

65 McIntosh *Feminism & Materialism* pp. 263–4

2 The contributions of the modern family to male violence

1 M. Poster *Critical Theory of the Family* London: Pluto Press, 1982, p. 155 and p. 164

2 ibid. p. 171

3 M. Bittman *What's Modern About the Modern Family?* Paper presented to T.A.S.A. Conference, La Trobe University, Melbourne, 8–12 December 1989, p. 12

4   ibid. p. 15
5   Poster *Critical Theory of the Family* pp. 171–4
6   ibid. p. 144
7   ibid. p. 143
8   P. Laslett quoted in M. Hirsch *Women and Violence* New York: Van Nostrand Reinhold, p. 174
9   R. Dobash and R. Dobash 'Community Response to Violence Against Wives: Charivari, Abstract Justice and Patriarchy' *Social Problems* 28 (5), 1981, pp. 563–81
10 J. Pahl (ed.) *Private Violence & Public Policy. The Needs of Battered Women & the Response of the Public Services* London: Routledge & Kegan Paul, 1985, p. 15
11 ibid. p. 19
12 D. Gil 'Societal Violence & Violence in Families' in J. Eekelaar and N. Katz (eds) *Family Violence an International and Inter-disciplinary Study* Toronto: Butterworths, 1978, p. 16
13 See Mike Donaldson's discussion around these issues, 'Labouring Men: Love, Sex & Strife' *Australian and New Zealand Journal of Sociology* 23 (2), 165–84
14 M. Straus 'Wife-beating: How Common and Why' in Eekelaar & Katz *Family Violence* p. 43
15 ibid. p. 43
16 ibid. p. 44
17 M. Straus 'A Sociological Perspective on the Prevention & Treatment of Wifebeating' in M. Roy (ed.) *Battered Women* New York: Van Nostrand, 1977, p. 212
18 ibid. p. 211
19 cf. C. Delphy and D. Leonard 'Class Analysis, Gender Analysis & the Family' in R. Crompton and M. Mann (eds) *Gender & Stratification* Oxford: Basil Blackwell, 1986, pp. 62–3
20 Straus *Family Violence* pp. 208–9
21 L. Feldman 'Sex Roles and Family Dynamics' in F. Walsh (ed.) *Normal Family Processes* New York: Guilford Press, 1985, p. 345
22 ibid. p. 355
23 ibid. p. 357
24 J. Rubin and B. Brown *The Social Psychology of Bargaining & Negotiation* New York: Academic Press, 1975, p. 173
25 Feldman *Normal Family Processes* p. 359
26 ibid. p. 360
27 ibid. p. 358
28 ibid. p. 359
29 ibid. p. 361
30 M. Meade *Bitching* St Albans: Granada Publishing, 1976, p. 148. The concept of bitching has a male bias built into it. Even though Marion Meade uncovers some of the serious issues behind bitching, she too uses the word in the sense of an attack on a defenceless man. Thus she fails to recognise the gendered power inequalities which do not allow women to take the direct or active approach to problem solving. Bitching and nagging are some few devices that women have permission to use. They are powerless in the real sense; and when women do resort to these practices they are put down, labelled and blamed for doing so.

31   L. Feldman 'Sex Roles and Family Dynamics' p. 362
32   I. Frieze, J. Parsons, P. Johnson, D. Ruble and G. Zellman *Women & Sex Roles. A Social Psychological Perspective* New York: W.W. Norton, 1978, p. 226
33   Feldman *Normal Family Processes* p. 363
34   See Dorothy Dinnerstein's creative discussion of such polarities in *The Rocking of the Cradle, and the Ruling of the World* London: Souvenir Press, 1978, p. 38
35   The heterosexist assumption built into this belief is so profound that it is hardly ever questioned. Why should a female be the *only* potential satisfier of male sexual needs? Masturbation as a sexual practice remains very much undercover and outside discussions of 'normal' sexuality. Masturbation of course avoids power inequalities, putting on another and aggression. On these grounds (and others) it should be a heavily endorsed sexual practice, particularly for teenagers with a strong sex drive and underdeveloped interpersonal skills.
36   See P. Blumstein and P. Schwartz *American Couples. Money. Work. Sex*, New York: William Morrow, 1983, pp. 206–14. This data derives from 3600 husbands and a similar number of wives, as well as 650 cohabiting males and a like number of females. Fifty per cent of husbands are the usual sex initiators, 39 per cent of male cohabitors, 15 per cent of female cohabitors and 12 per cent of wives. The gay men and lesbian figures from a sample of 1900 of the former and 1600 of latter indicate a more equal sharing of initiating sexual activities with 31 per cent from each group deeming themselves the primary initiator.
37   Tom Cayler quoted in M. Kimmel, (ed.) *Men Confront Pornography* New York: Crown Publishers, 1990, p. 52
38   L. Feldman p. 364
39   Andy Metcalf is an insightful male who is sufficiently self-confident and brave to put such honest levels of self-awareness into print. Quoted in A. Metcalf & M. Humphries (eds) *The Sexuality of Men* London: Pluto Press, 1985, p. 101
40   H. Goldberg *The Hazards of Being Male* New York: Signet, 1976, p. 48
41   A. Rosenbaum and K. O'Leary 'Marital Violence: Characteristics of Abusive Couples' *Journal of Consulting & Clinical Psychology* 49 (1), 1981, p. 67
42   D. McIntyre 'Domestic Violence: A Case of the Disappearing Victim? *Australian Journal of Family Therapy* 5 (4), 1984, p. 256
43   ibid. p. 256. Wini Breines and Linda Gordon quoted.
44   B. English and R. King *Families in Australia* Sydney: Bridge Printery, 1983, p. 46
45   J. Finn 'The Relationship between Sex Role Attitudes & Attitudes Supporting Marital Violence' *Sex Roles* vol. 14 (5/6), 1986, p. 235
46   English and King *Families in Australia* Table 3.11, p. 45
47   ibid. table 3.12, p. 51
48   ibid. table 3.13, p. 52
49   See also R. Scott and L. Tetreault, 'Attitudes of Rapists and other Violent Offenders towards Women' *The Journal of Social Psychology* 127 (4), 375–80
50   English and King *Families in Australia* p. 189

51 Bittman *What's Modern About The Modern Family* p. 9. He cites his own previous study which revealed that men's unique contributions to the household (sic) were car and pool maintenance. He and Frances Lovejoy discerned that not only do married women with young children do much more housework than unmarried women without children; but also more than single mothers.

52 W. Hollway ' "I Just Wanted to Kill a Woman." Why? The Ripper and Male Sexuality' in Feminist Review Collective (eds) *Sexuality: A Reader* London: Virago, 1987, p. 124.

3 The contributions of male gender construction and reproduction to male violence

1 D. Morgan *The Family, Politics and Social Theory* London: Routledge and Kegan Paul, 1985, p. 237. See also C. Burton *Subordination. Feminism & Social Theory* Sydney: Allen & Unwin, 1985, p. 89 and A. Game & R. Pringle *Gender at Work* Sydney: Allen & Unwin, 1983, p. 93

2 A. Giddens *Central Problems in Social Theory. Action, Structure & Contradictions in Social Analysis* London: Macmillan, 1979, p. 58

3 H. Kaplan and B. Sadock *Modern Synopsis of Comprehensive Textbook of Psychiatry/IV* Baltimore: Williams & Wilkins, 1985

4 N. Chodorow 'Family Structure & Feminine Personality' in M. Rosaldo and L. Lamphere (eds) *Woman, Culture & Society* California: Stanford University Press, 1974, p. 43

5 ibid. p. 45

6 S. Freud *New Introductory Lectures on Psychoanalysis*, The Pelican Freud Library, vol. 2 (trans. J. Strachey) London: Cox & Wyman, 1977, p. 98

7 Chodorow, *Women, Culture & Society*, p. 48

8 See, for example, E. Person 'Sexuality as the Mainstay of Identity: Psychoanalytic Perspectives' in C. Stimpson and E. Person (eds) *Women, Sex and Sexuality* Chicago: University of Chicago Press, 1980, p. 49

9 N. Chodorow *The Reproduction of Mothering. Psychoanalysis and the Sociology of Gender* Berkeley: University of California Press, 1978, p. 111

10 Chodorow *Woman, Culture & Society* p. 52, footnote

11 Chodorow *The Reproduction of Mothering* p. 115

12 G. Rubin 'The Traffic in Women: Notes on the "Political Economy" of Sex' in R. Reiter (ed.) *Toward an Anthropology of Women* New York: Monthly Review Press, 1975, p. 185

13 Chodorow *The Reproduction of Mothering* p. 117

14 M. Krull *Freud & His Father* London: W W Norton, 1987

15 P. Slater 'Parental Role Differentiation' in R. Coser (ed.) *The Family. It's Structures & Functions* New York: St Martins Press, 1974, p. 270

16 N. Chodorow (1978), pp. 175–6

17 See Feldman, as well as V. Seidler 'Fear & Intimacy' in A. Metcalf and M. Humphries (eds) *The Sexuality of Men* London: Pluto Press, 1985

18 Chodorow *The Reproduction of Mothering* p. 185

19 ibid. p. 175

20 Talcott Parsons cited in J. Toby 'Violence and the Masculine Ideal' in S. Steinmetz and M. Straus (eds) *Violence in the Family* New York: Harper & Row, 1974

21 However John Steley's discussion of sexually abusive phone callers supports this idea, *Australian Journal of Marriage & Family*, vol. 11 (1), 1990, p. 22. Dorothy Ullian 'Why Boys will be Boys' *American Journal of Orthopsychiatry* 51 (3), 1981, p. 498 also makes such a claim.

22 Ullian *American Journal of Orthopsychiatry* 51 (3), p. 495

23 ibid. pp. 494–6

24 S. Miller *Men & Friendship* Bath: Gateway, 1983, p. 135

25 E. Person p. 50

26 D. Martin (1981), p. 62

27 See M. Fasteau *The Male Machine* New York: Delta, 1975, pp. 212–3 and L. Feldman p. 108

28 Ullian *American Journal of Orthopsychiatry* 51 (3), p. 498

29 M. Fasteau, *The Male Machine* p. 37

30 J. Garrett-Gooding and R. Senter 'Attitudes & Acts of Sexual Agression on a University Campus' *Sociological Inquiry* 57 (4), 1987, p. 367

31 Hartley quoted in Fasteau *The Male Machine* p. 39

32 N. Chodorow *The Reproduction of Mothering* p. 176

33 G. Lewis *Real Men Like Violence* Sydney: Kangaroo Press, 1983, p. 85

34 Chodorow *The Reproduction of Mothering* p. 175

35 Cited in Fasteau *The Male Machine* p. 212. See also R. Conway *The End of the Stupour?* Melbourne: Macmillan, 1984, pp. 70–1

36 Read S. Freud *Civilization and its Discontents* revised and edited by J. Strachey, London: Hogarth Press, 1979, p. 342, closely

37 T. Ryan in Metcalf & Humphries *The Sexuality of Men* p. 15

38 R. Whitehurst in Steinmetz & Straus *Violence in the Family* p. 79

39 Kaplan and Sadock *Modern Synopsis of Comprehensive Textbook of Psychiatry/IV* p. 80

40 For conscious evidence of this bias see S. Freud *On Sexuality* Harmondsworth: Penguin, 1979, p. 342

41 Chodorow *The Reproduction of Mothering* p. 193

42 ibid. p. 192

43 J. Fleming *Stopping Wife Abuse* New York: Anchor, 1979, p. 393

44 M. Roy (ed.) *Battered Women. A Psycho-sociological Study of Domestic Violence* New York: Van Nostrand Reinhold, 1977

45 A. Tolson *The Limits of Masculinity* London: Tavistock, 1977, p. 25

46 ibid. p. 25

47 ibid. p. 31

48 ibid. p. 37

49 ibid. p. 38

50 ibid. p. 39

51 See Ryan *The Sexuality of Men*, cases Dave and Ralph, for graphic examples of the omission of the father's relationship with his son pp. 22–5

52 C. Weedon *Feminist Practice and Poststructuralist Theory* Oxford: Basil Blackwell, 1987, has also noted the significance of the concept of positional identification

4 Male violence, female target

1   L. Walker *The Battered Woman* New York: Harper & Row, 1979, p. 36. For recent Australian recognition of similar characteristics see D. Wehner 'Working With Violent Men. Issues, Programs & Training' in S. Hatty (ed.) *Proceedings, National Conference on Domestic Violence* Canberra: Australian Institute of Criminology, 1986

2   M. Pagelow *Woman—Battering. Victims and their Experiences* Beverly Hills: Sage, 1981, p. 103

3   S. Epstein 'The Self-concept' in E. Staub (ed.) *Personality: Basic Issues & Current Research* New York: Prentice-Hall, 1980, pp. 225–6

4   P. Amato *Children in Australian Families* Sydney: Prentice-Hall, 1987, pp. 98–9. J. Buri, P. Kirchner and J. Walsh make similar associations in 'Familial Correlates of Self-Esteem in Young American Adults' *The Journal of Social Psychology* 127 (6), 1987, p. 585

5   E. Jacobsen 5th edn *The Self & the Object World* International Universities Press, 1980, p. 130

6   B. Pelham and W. Swann 'From Self-Conceptions to Self-Worth: On the Sources & Structures of Global Self-Esteem' *Journal of Personality & Social Psychology* vol. 57 (4), 1989, pp. 672–80

7   E. Fromm *The Art of Loving* London: Allen & Unwin, 1982

8   See, for example, D. Currie 'A Toronto Model' *Social Work With Groups*, vol. 6:179; E. Gondolf *Men Who Batter*, Holmes Beach: Learning Publications, 1985, p. 28; A. Walker-Hooper 'Domestic Violence: Assessing the Problem' in C. Warner (ed.) *Conflict Intervention in Social & Domestic Violence* London: Prentice-Hall, 1981, p. 59

9   R. May *Power & Innocence* New York: Fontana, 1976, p. 23

10 A. Storr Introduction to J. Eekelaar and S. Katz (eds) *Family Violence. An International & Interdisciplinary Study* Toronto: Butterworths, 1978, p. 7. See also S. Taubman 'Beyond the Bravado: Sex Roles & the Exploitive Male' *Social Work* January-February, vol. 31 (1), 1986, p. 14

11 M. Messner 'The Meaning of Success: The Athletic Experience & the Development of Male Identity' in H. Brod (ed.) *The Making of Masculinities* Boston: Allen & Unwin, 1987, p. 194

12 M. Fasteau *The Male Machine* New York: Delta, 1975, pp. 212–3

13 D. Martin *Battered Wives* San Francisco: Volcano Press, 1981, p. 62

14 D. Ullian 'Why Boys will be Boys' *American Journal of Orthopsychiatry* 51 (3), 1981, p. 496

15 ibid. p. 498

16 ibid. p. 495

17 Ruth Hartley's 1950s studies cited in Fasteau *The Male Machine* p. 39

18 See R. Connell *Which Way is Up?* Sydney: Allen & Unwin, p. 20

19 Fasteau *The Male Machine* p. 105

20 Bob Connell makes similar comments in *Which Way is Up?* p. 18

21 Messner *The Making of Masculinities* p. 196

22 P. Willis *Learning to Labour. How Working Class Kids get Working Class Jobs* Aldershot: Gower Publishing, 1977, p. 150

23 A. Game and R. Pringle *Gender at Work* Sydney: Allen & Unwin, 1983, p. 15

24 J. Hearn 'Men's Sexuality at Work' in A. Metcalf and M. Humphries (eds) *The Sexuality of Men* London: Pluto Press, 1985, p. 121
25 ibid. pp. 122–3
26 M. Pagelow *Family Violence* New York: Praeger, 1984, p. 98
27 M. Donaldson 'Labouring Men: Love, Sex & Strife' *A & N.Z. Journal of Sociology*, vol. 23 (2), 1987, pp. 167–8
28 Willis *Learning to Labour* pp. 148–9
29 Chamberlain cited in Donaldson *A. & NZ Journal of Sociology* vol. 23 (2), 1987, p. 167
30 ibid. p. 170, Williams cited
31 ibid. p. 171, Stanley cited
32 G. Lewis *Real Men Like Violence*, Sydney: Kangaroo Press, 1983, p. 86
33 Pagelow *Family Violence* p. 98
34 R. Lemle and M. Mishkind 'Alcohol & Masculinity' *Journal of Substance Abuse Treatment* vol. 6, 1989, p. 214
35 ibid. p. 213
36 ibid. pp. 214–5
37 ibid. pp. 215–6
38 ibid. p. 216
39 For example, D. Coleman and M. Straus 'Alcohol Abuse & Family Violence' in E. Gottheil *et al* (eds) *Alcohol, Drug Abuse & Aggression* Springfield: Charles Thomas, 1983; G. Kantor and M. Straus 'The "Drunken Bum" Theory of Wife Beating' *Social Problems* vol. 34 (3), 1987, pp. 213–30; V. Van Hasselt, R. Morrison and A. Bellack 'Alcohol Use in Wife Abusers & their Spouses' *Addictive Behaviors* vol. 10 1985, pp. 127–35
40 M. Bard and J. Zacker 'Assaultiveness & Alcohol Use in Family Disputes. Police Perceptions' *Criminology* vol. 12 (3), 1974, pp. 281–92
41 Kantor and Straus make similar associations in *Social Problems* vol. 34 (3), 1987, p. 225
42 R. Dyer 'Male Sexuality in the Media' in A. Metcalf and M. Humphries (eds) *The Sexuality of Men* p. 28
43 P. Filene 'The Secrets of Men's History' in H. Brod (ed.) *The Making of Masculinities* p. 112
44 T. Eardley 'Violence & Sexuality' in A. Metcalf and M. Humphries (eds) *The Sexuality of Men* pp. 100–1
45 See A. Metcalf & M. Humphries (eds) *The Sexuality of Men*—Eardley p. 105, Metcalf p. 101, Seidler, p. 161. Lenore Walker also notes the confusion of these needs in *The Battered Woman Syndrome* New York: Springer, 1984, p. 55
46 V. Seidler 'Fear & Intimacy' in A. Metcalf, and M. Humphries (eds) *The Sexuality of Men* p. 161
47 Erich Fromm cited in D. Martin *Battered Wives* p. 69. I have changed the pronouns in the first two sentences quoted to the female gender.
48 G. Ryan, S. Lane, J. Davis and C. Isaac 'Juvenile Sex Offenders: 'Development & Correction' *Child Abuse & Neglect* vol. 11 1987, pp. 385–95
49 ibid. pp. 390–1
50 ibid. pp. 391–2
51 ibid. p. 392

52 Regarding batterers, see Currie *Social Work With Groups* vol. 6 p. 179;
    A. Newton 'Violent Marriages *Australian Journal of Family Therapy*, 3
    (1) 1981, pp. 29–30; Walker-Hooper *Conflict Intervention* pp. 58–9;
    Wehner *Proceedings, National Conference on Domestic Violence* p.
    313; J. Weitzman and K. Dreen 'Wife Beating: A View of the Marital
    Dyad' *Social Casework*, May 1982, pp. 259–65
        Regarding incest perpetrators, see A. Burgess 'Intra-familial Sexual
    Abuse' in J. Campbell, and J. Humphreys (eds) *Nursing Care of Victims
    of Family Violence* Reston: Reston Publishing, 1984, p. 200; V. Drake,
    'Therapy With Victims of Abuse' in C. Beck, R. Rawlins and S. Wil-
    liams (eds) *Mental Health—Psychiatric Nursing* St Louis: C.V. Mosby,
    1984, p. 937; B. Star *Helping the Abuser* New York: Family Service,
    Association, 1983, p. 35
        Regarding rapists, R. Rada *Clinical Aspects of the Rapist* New York:
    Grune & Statton, 1978, cites a study of 100 rapists which concludes
    that 'rape is an expression of hostility by a male who feels weak,
    inadequate and dependent' (p. 31). He also discusses rapists' feelings of
    sexual inadequacy, pp. 39–40
53 See P. Filene on Woodrow Wilson's 'secret' overdependence on his
    wives; B. Rounsaville 'Theories in Marital Violence' *Victimology* vol. 3
    (1–2) 1978, p. 20; Walker *The Battered Woman Syndrome* p. 39
54 J. Foss 'The Paradoxical Nature of Family Relationships & Family
    Conflict' in M. Straus and G. Hotaling (eds) *The Social Causes of
    Husband-Wife Violence* Minneapolis: University of Minnesota Press,
    1980, pp. 117–9
55 L. Feldman 'Sex Roles and Family Dynamics' in F. Walsh (ed.) *Normal
    Family Processes* New York: Guilford Press, 1985; S. Jourard *The
    Transparent Self*, New York: Van Nostrand, 1971; J. Pleck *The Myth
    of Masculinity* Cambridge: Massachusetts Institute of Technology Press,
    1981
56 Hoffman *The Myth of Masculinity* p. 148
57 H. Goldberg *The Hazards of Being Male* New York: Signet, 1976, p. 53
58 D. Russell cited in J. Pleck *The Myth of Masculinity* p. 146
59 W. Hollway ' "I Just Wanted to Kill a Woman". Why? The Ripper &
    Male Sexuality' in Feminist Review Collective *Sexuality A Reader* Lon-
    don: Virago, 1987, p. 129; M. Roy (ed.) *Battered Women* New York:
    Van Nostrand, 1977, p. 40; Walker-Hooper *Conflict Intervention* p. 62
60 Walker *The Battered Woman Syndrome*
61 ibid. pp. 48–9
62 Seidler *Sexuality of Men* p. 161
63 Martin *Battered Wives* pp. 58–60; Walker in *The Battered Woman
    Syndrome* p. 50, found that over 50 per cent of battered women in her
    sample of 400 said the batterer was 'always' jealous in contrast to 6 per
    cent women with a nonviolent spouse; Wehner *Proceedings, National
    Conference on Domestic Violence* p. 313
64 Rounsaville *Victimology* vol. 3 (1–2), p. 21
65 Currie *Social Work With Groups* vol. 6 p. 185; Newton *Australian
    Journal of Family Therapy* 3 (1), p. 31; Weitzman and Dreen *Social
    Casework* May 1982, p. 263
66 Currie *Social Work With Groups* vol. 6 p. 185; M. Elbow, 'Theoretical

Considerations of Violent Marriages' *Social Casework* November 1977, pp. 515–26; B. Star *Helping the Abuser. Intervening Effectively in Family Violence* New York: Family Service Association of America, 1983. p. 34.

5 What can be done to prevent male violence towards females

1 For example, M. Girdler, 'Domestic Violence: Social Solutions' in C. O'Donnell and J. Craney *Family Violence in Australia* Canberra: Australian Institute of Criminology 1982; D. Martin *Battered Wives* San Francisco: Volcano Press, 1981, pp. 187–92; J. Scutt *Even in the Best of Homes: Violence in the Family* Ringwood: Penguin, 1983, pp. 276–84

2 See D. Knuckey 'Equality at Work Remains Elusive' *The Weekend Australian* 3 February 1990 p. 46. According to statistics from the Australian Bureau of Statistics, women working full time in 1989 earned 79 per cent of the average earnings of men. The average weekly total earnings of full-time plus part-time women was 65 per cent of the average for men. The workforce continues to be highly segregated, with women clustered in lower paying jobs. Only 24 per cent of managers and administrators were women.

3 S. Jackson 'The Social Context of Rape' *Women's Studies International Quarterly* vol. 1, p. 37

4 cf. R. Connell *Gender & Power*, Sydney: Allen & Unwin, 1987, p. 100

5 Girdler *Family Violence in Australia*, p. 150

6 M. Straus 'A Sociological Perspective on the Prevention & Treatment of Wifebeating' in M. Roy (ed.) *Battered Women* New York: Van Nostrand, 1977, p. 210. See also A. Sanson and M. Prior 'Growing Up in a Violent World' *Network* 5 (2), 1989, pp. 16–26

7 J. Edleson 'Working With Men Who Batter' *Social Work* May–June 1984, p. 240

8 Connell *Gender & Power* p. 231

9 Jackson *Women's Studies International Quarterly* vol. 1, p. 37

10 D. Wehner 'Working With Violent Men' in S. Hatty (ed.) *Proceedings, National Conference on Domestic Violence* p. 312

11 B. Hall, L. Lamont, J. MacKintosh and W. St John 'A Guidebook for Teaching Parenting' is summarized and discussed in *The Australian Nurses Journal*, vol. 17, No. 4 1987, pp. 52–5

12 A. Burns and J. Goodnow 'Violence Against Children' (Chapter 5) of *Children & Families in Australia* Sydney: Allen & Unwin, 1985, p. 210

13 L. Baron and M. Straus 'Four Theories of Rape: A Macrosociological Analysis' *Social Problems* vol. 34 (5), 1987, p. 483

14 Jackson *Women's Studies International Quarterly* vol. 1, p. 35

15 *ibid.* p. 31

16 R. Conway *The End of the Stupour?* Melbourne: Macmillan, 1984, p. 110

17 ibid. p. 75–7

18 R. Fletcher 'Non-Sexist Education for Boys' *Education* 30 June 1988, p. 24

19 See Baron and Straus *Social Problems* vol. 34 (5), 1987, p. 469, for example

20 Jackson *Women's Studies International Quarterly* vol. 1, p. 34

21   cf. P. Amato *Children in Australian Families: The Growth of Competence* Sydney: Prentice Hall, 1987, p. 240
22   See J. Buri *et al* 'Familial Correlates of Self-Esteem in Young American Adults' *The Journal of Social Psychology* 127 (6), 1987, p. 585
23   Jackson *Women's Studies International Quarterly* vol. 1, p. 27
24   Straus *Battered Women*. See pp. 232–3 for his summary of political-social interventions.

6 Conclusions

 1   D. McIntyre 'Domestic Violence: A Case of the Disappearing Victim' *Australian Journal of Family Therapy* 5 (4), 1984, 249–58
 2   C. Caine and T. Caine cited in L. Phelps 'Patriarchy and Capitalism in Essays from Quest, *Building Feminist Theory*, New York: Longman, 1981, p. 170
 3   D. Gil 'Societal Violence and Violence in Families' in J. Eekelaar and N. Katz (eds) *Family Violence. An International & Interdisciplinary Study* Toronto: Butterworths, 1978
 4   D. Lester 'A Cross-Culture Study of Wife Abuse' *Aggressive Behavior* vol. 6, 1980, p. 361
 5   D. Kalmuss and M. Straus 'Wife Marital Dependency & Wife Abuse' *Journal of Marriage & the Family* vol. 44 (2) 1982, p. 277
 6   M. Fasteau *The Male Machine* New York: Delta, 1975
 7   From L. Feldman 'Sex Roles & Family Dynamics' in F. Walsh (ed.) *Normal Family Processes* New York: Guilford Press, 1985
 8   D. Gittins *The Family in Question* Basingstoke: Macmillan, 1986, p. 70
 9   M. Poster *Critical Theory of the Family* London: Pluto, 1982
10   See B. English and R. King *Families in Australia* Sydney: Bridge, 1983; L. Scanzoni and J. Scanzoni *Men, Women & Change* New York: McGraw-Hill, 1976
11   L. Scanzoni and J. Scanzoni *Men, Women and Change. A Sociology of Marriage and Family* New York: McGraw-Hill, 1976, p. 342
12   See B. English and R. King *Families in Australia* Sydney: Bridge Printers, 1983, for Australian evidence. See J. Finn 'The Relationship between Sex Role Attitudes & Attitudes supporting Marital Violence' *Sex Roles* vol. 14 (5/6), 1986, p. 241 for a more specific and recent study of undergraduate students.
13   Fasteau *The Male Machine* p. 116
14   C. Burton *Subordination* Sydney: Allen & Unwin, 1985
15   Fasteau *The Male Machine* p. 91
16   ibid. p. 96
17   W. Breines and L. Gordon 'The New Scholarship on Family Violence' *Signs* vol. 8 (3), 1983, p. 492
18   ibid. p. 530
19   cf. R. Connell *Gender & Power* Sydney: Allen & Unwin, 1987, p. 114
20   N. Denzin 'Toward a Phenomenology of Domestic, Family Violence' *American Journal of Sociology* vol. 90 (3), 1984, pp. 489–90
21   ibid. pp. 488–9
22   E. Person 'Sexuality as the Mainstay of Identity' in C. Stimpson & E. Person (eds) *Women, Sex & Sexuality* Chicago: University of Chicago Press, 1980
23   Adler cited in Connell *Gender & Power* p. 199

24 According to data from New South Wales committal hearings for sexual offences, 75 per cent of the defendants were known to the complainant. In a 1983 study in South Australia of 450 alleged sexual assault offenders (from minor indecency acts to brutal rapes), 58 per cent of the assailants were known to the victim. National Committee on Violence *Violence. Directions for Australia* Canberra: Australian Institute of Criminology, 1990, pp. 30–1

25 Connell *Gender & Power* p. 92

26 For example, J. Alexander *et al* (eds) *The Macro-Micro Link* Berkeley: University of California Press, 1986
   J. Chafetz 'The Gender Division of Labor and the Reproduction of Female Disadvantage' *Journal of Family Issues* vol. 9 (1), 1988, pp. 108–31
   A. Giddens *The Constitution of Society: Introduction to the Theory of Structuration* Berkeley: University of California Press, 1984

27 M. Poster *Critical Theory of the Family* London: Pluto Press, 1982

28 N. Chodorow 'Mothering, Male Dominance & Capitalism' in Z. Eisentein (ed.) *Capitalism, Patriarchy & the Case for Socialist Feminism* New York: Monthly Review Press, 1979

29 N. Chodorow *The Reproduction of Mothering. Psychoanalysis & the Sociology of Gender* Berkeley: University of California Press, 1978

30 See M. Girdler 'Domestic Violence: Social Solutions' in C. O'Donnel & J. Craney (eds) *Family Violence in Australia* Melbourne: Longman Cheshire, 1982
   M. Straus 'A Sociological Perspective on the Prevention & Treatment of Wife Beating' in M. Roy (ed.) *Battered Women* New York: Van Nostrand, 1977
   C. Swift 'Preventing Family Violence: Family-Focused Programs' in M. Lystad (ed.) *Violence in the Home. Inter-disciplinary Perspectives* New York: Brunner/Mazel, 1986

31 F. Baum *et al* 'Preventing Family Violence: The Evaluation of a Group for Men who are Violent towards their Partners' *Australian Journal of Sex, Marriage & Family* 8 (4), 1987, pp. 173–83; S. Hatty 'On the Reproduction of Misogyny: The Therapeutic Management of Violence Against Women' in S. Hatty (ed.) *Proceedings, National Conference on Domestic Violence* Canberra: Australian Institute of Criminology, November 1985; D. Wehner 'Working With Violent Men. Issues, Programs & Training in S. Hatty *Proceedings, National Conference on Domestic Violence* Canberra: Australian Institute of Criminology, 1986

32 C. Burton *Subordination. Feminism & Social Theory* Sydney: Allen & Unwin, 1985, p. xiv

33 Connell pp. 201–5

34 C. Weedon (1987) *Feminist Practice & Post-structuralist Theory*, Oxford, Basil Blackwell, p. 59, my emphasis. Weedon is the only author I am aware of who has recognized the explanatory power of the concepts personal identification and positional identification.

35 See Connell *Gender & Power* p. 204

Bibliography

MALE VIOLENCE

The Age (9 March 1988) 'Survey Finds Many Accept Widespread Violence in the Home', p. 1

The Australian (9 March 1988) '20 Percent Accept Wife Bashing', p. 1

Bard, M. and Zacker, J. (1974) 'Assaultiveness and Alcohol Use in Family Disputes. Police Perceptions' *Criminology* Vol. 12 no. 3, pp. 281–92

Baron, L. and Straus, M. (1987) 'Four Theories of Rape: A Macrosociologic Analysis' *Social Problems* Vol. 34 no. 5, pp. 467–88

Baum, F., Brand, R., Colley, D. and Cooke, R. (1987) 'Preventing Family Violence: The Evaluation of a Group for Men Who Are Violent Towards Their Partners' *Australian Journal of Sex, Marriage & Family* 8 (4), pp. 173–83

Bell, D. (1984) 'The Police Response to Domestic Violence: An Exploratory Study' *Police Studies* Vol. 7 no. 1, pp. 23–30

Bentovim, A., Elton, A., Hildebrand, J., Tranter, M., and Vizard, E. eds (1988) *Child Sexual Abuse Within the Family: Assessment & Treatment* London: Wright

Bernard, J. L. and Bernard, M. L. (1984) 'The Abusive Male Seeking Treatment: Jekyll and Hyde' *Family Relations* Vol. 33 no. 4, pp. 543–7

Borkowski, M., Murch, M. and Walker, V. (1983) *Marital Violence. The Community Response* London: Tavistock

Breines, W. and Gordon, L. (1983) 'The New Scholarship on Family Violence' *Signs* Vol. 8 no. 3, pp. 490–531

Browning, J. and Dutton, D. (1986) 'Assessment of Wife Assault with the Conflict Tactics Scale: Using Couple Data to Quantify the Differential Reporting Effect' *Journal of Marriage & the Family* 48, pp. 375–9

Burgess, A. (1984) 'Intra-familial Sexual Abuse in Campbell' in J. and J. Humphreys eds *Nursing Care of Victims of Family Violence* Reston: Reston Publishing Co.

Burns, A. and Goodnow, J. (1985) 'Violence Against Children' in A. Burns and J. Goodnow *Children & Families in Australia* Sydney: Allan & Unwin

Campbell, J. and Humphreys, J. (1984) *Nursing Care of Victims of Family Violence* Reston: Prentice-Hall

Carlson, B. (1977) 'Battered Women & their Assailants' *Social Work* Vol. 22, pp. 455–60

Carmen, E., Rieker, P. and Mills, T. 'Victims of Violence and Psychiatric Illness' *American Journal of Psychiatry* March 1984, 141 (3), pp. 378–83

Coleman, D. and Straus, M. (1983) 'Alcohol Abuse and Family Violence' in E. Gottheil, K. Druley, T. Skoloda and H. Waxman eds *Alcohol, Drug Abuse and Aggression* Springfield: Charles Thomas

Cordell, M. (1986) 'New Ways to Deal With the Domestic' *Sydney Morning Herald* 13 September 1986, p. 13

Currie, D. (1983) 'A Toronto Model' *Social Work with Groups* Vol. 6, pp. 179–88

Denzin, N. (1984) 'Toward A Phenomenology of Domestic, Family Violence' *American Journal of Sociology* Vol. 9 no. 3, pp. 483–513

Deschner, J. (1984) *The Hitting Habit* New York: The Free Press

Dobash, R. and Dobash, R.E. 'Community Response to Violence Against Wives: Charivari, Abstract Justice and Patriarchy' *Social Problems* Vol. 28, (5), June 1981, pp. 5630–81

Dobash, R. and Dobash R. (1984) 'The Nature & Antecedents of Violent Events' *British Journal of Criminology* Vol. 24 no. 3, pp. 269–88

Dobash, R. E. and Dobash, R. (1980) *Violence Against Wives* London: Open Books

Doherty, J. (1983) *Self-Esteem, Anxiety and Dependency in Men Who Batter Women* Education Doctorate (on microfilm), Boston University

Drake, V. (1984) 'Therapy With Victims of Abuse' in C. Beck, R. Rawlins and S. Williams eds *Mental Health—Psychiatric Nursing. A Holistic Life-Cycle Approach* St. Louis: C. V. Mosby

Eardly, T. (1985) 'Violence and Sexuality' in A. Metcalf and M. Humphries eds *The Sexuality of Men* London: Pluto Press

Eberle, P. (1982) 'Alcohol Abusers and Non-Users: A Discriminant Analysis of Differences Between Two Subgroups of Batterers' *Journal of Health & Social Behavior* Vol. 23, pp. 260–71

Edleson, J. (1984) 'Working With Men Who Batter' *Social Work* May–June, pp. 237–42

Edwards, A. (1987) 'Male Violence in Feminist Theory: An Analysis of the Changing Conceptions of Sex/Gender Violence and Male Dominance' in J. Hanmer and M. Maynard (eds) *Women, Violence and Social Control* London: Macmillan

Elbow, M. 'Theoretical Considerations of Violent Marriages' *Social Casework* November 1977, pp. 515–26

Ferraro, K. and Johnson, J. (1983) 'How Women Experience Battering: The Process of Victimization' *Social Problems* Vol. 30 no. 3, pp. 325–39

Finkelhor, D. (1983) 'Family Abuse' in D. Finkelhor, R. Gelles, G. Hotaling and M. Straus eds *The Dark Side of Families* Beverly Hills: Sage

Finn, J. (1986) 'The Relationship Between Sex Role Attitudes and Attitudes Supporting Marital Violence' *Sex Roles* Vol. 14 nos. 5/6, pp. 235–44

Fleming, J. B. (1979) *Stopping Wife Abuse* New York: Anchor

Flynn, J. 'Recent Findings Related to Wife Abuse' *Social Casework* January 1977, pp. 13–20

Foss, J. (1980) 'The Paradoxical Nature of Family Relationships and Family Conflict' in M. Straus and G. Hotaling eds *The Social Causes of Husband-Wife Violence* Minneapolis: University of Minnesota Press

Gaquin, D. (1977) 'Spouse Abuse: Data from the National Crime Survey' *Victimology* Vol. 2, pp. 632–43

Garrett-Gooding, J. and Senter, R. (1987) 'Attitudes and Acts of Sexual Aggression on a University Campus' *Sociological Inquiry* 57 (4), pp. 348–71

Gelles, R. (1978) 'Violence in the American Family' in J. P. Martin ed. *Violence and the Family* New York: John Wiley

Gelles, R. and Straus, M. 'Determinants of Violence in the Family: Toward a

Theoretical Integration' in W. Burr *et al* eds (1979) *Contemporary Theories About the Family* Vol. I, New York: Free Press

Gentemann, K. Wife Beating: Attitude of a Non-Clinical Population' *Victimology* Vol. 9 1984 (1), pp. 109–19

Gil, D. (1978) 'Societal Violence & Violence in Families' in J. Eekelaar and N. Katz eds *Family Violence. An International & Interdisciplinary Study* Toronto: Butterworths

Gil, D. (1986) 'Sociocultural Aspects of Domestic Violence' in Mary Lystad ed. *Violence in the Home: Interdisciplinary Perspectives* New York: Brunner/Mazel

Girdler, M. (1982) 'Domestic Violence: Social Solutions' in C. O'Donnell & J. Craney, *Family Violence in Australia* Canberra: Australian Institute of Criminology

Gondolf, E. (1985) *Men Who Batter: An Integrated Approach For Stopping Wife Abuse* Holmes Beach: Learning Publications

Goode, W. 'Force & Violence in the Family' *Journal of Marriage & the Family* November 1971, Vol. 33, pp. 624–36

Guerney, B. Waldo, M. and Firestone, L. (1987) 'Wife-Battering: A Theoretical Construct and Case Report' *The American Journal of Family Therapy* Vol. 15 No. 1, pp. 34–43

Hanmer, J. (1978) 'Violence & the Social Control of Women' in G. Littlejohn, B. Smart, J. Wakeford and N. Yuval-Davis eds *Power and the State* London: Croom Helm

Hartman, C. and Burgess, A. (1988) 'Rape Trauma & Treatment of the Victim' in F. Ochberg ed. *Post-Traumatic Therapy & Victims of Violence* New York: Brunner/Mazel

Hatty, S. (1986) 'On the Reproduction of Misogyny: The Therapeutic Management of Violence Against Women' in S. Hatty ed. *Proceedings, National Conference on Domestic Violence* Nov. 1985, Canberra: Australian Institute of Criminology

Hatty, S. 'Woman Battering as a Social Problem: The Denial of Injury' *Australian & New Zealand Journal of Sociology* March 1987, Vol. 23 (1), pp. 36–46

Healy, J. (1984) *After the Refuge: A Study of Battered Wives in Adelaide* Adelaide: Dept. for Community Welfare SA

Hendrix, M. (1981) 'Home is Where The Hell Is' *Family & Community Health* Vol. 4 August, pp. 53–9

Herman, J. (1988) 'Father-Daughter Incest' in F. Ochberg ed. *Post Traumatic Therapy & Victims of Violence* New York: Brunner/Mazel

Hilberman, E. and Munson, K. (1977–8) 'Sixty Battered Women' *Victimology* Vol. 2 nos. 3–4, pp. 460–70

Hirsch, M. F. (1981) 'To Love, Cherish and Batter' in M. F. Hirsch *Women and Violence* New York: Van Nostrand Reinhold

Hollway, W. (1987) ' "I Just Wanted to Kill a Woman". Why? The Ripper and Male Sexuality' in Feminist Review Collective eds *Sexuality: A Reader* London: Virago

Homer, M., Leonard A. and Taylor, P. (1985) 'Personal Relationships: Help and Hindrance' in N. Johnson ed. *Family Violence* London: Routledge & Kegan Paul

Jackson, S. (1978) 'The Social Context of Rape: Sexual Scripts & Motivation' *Women's Studies International Quarterly* 1, pp. 27–38

Jackson, S. and Rushton, P. 'Victims & Villains: Images of Women in Accounts of Family Violence' *Women's Studies International Forum* 1982, Vol. 5 (1), pp. 17–28

Johnson, N. ed. (1983) *Marital Violence* London: Routledge & Kegan Paul

Kalmuss, D. and Seltzer J. 'Continuity of Marital Behavior in Remarriage: The Case of Spouse Abuse' *Journal of Marriage & the Family* 48 (Feb. 1986), pp. 113–20

Kalmuss, D. and Straus, M. (1982) 'Wife's Marital Dependency & Wife Abuse' *Journal of Marriage & the Family* Vol. 44 no. 2, May, pp. 277–86

Kantor, G. and Straus, M. (1987) 'The "Drunken Bum" Theory of Wife Beating' *Social Problems* Vol. 34 no. 3, pp. 213–30

Knight, R. and Hatty, S. 'Theoretical & Methodological Perspectives on Domestic Violence: Implications for Social Action' *Australia Journal of Social Issues*, May 1987, 22 (2), pp. 452–64

Kurz, D. (1987) 'Emergency Department Responses to Battered Women: Resistance to Medicalization' *Social Problems* Vol. 34 no. 1, pp. 69–81

Lansdowne, R. (1985) 'Domestic Violence Legislation in New South Wales' *University of New South Wales, Law Journal* Vol. 8, pp. 80–105

Lester, D. (1980) A Cross-Culture Study of Wife Abuse, *Aggressive Behavior*, Vol. 6: 361–4

Lewis, G. (1983) *Real Men Like Violence* Sydney: Kangaroo Press

Loseke, D. and Cahill, S. (1984) 'The Social Construction of Deviance: Experts on Battered Women' *Social Problems* Vol. 31 no. 3, pp 296–310

Martin, D. (1981) *Battered Wives* San Francisco: Volcano Press

Masumura, W. (1979) 'Wife Abuse & Other Forms of Aggression' *Victimology* Vol. 4 (1), pp. 46–59

May, R. (1976) *Power and Innocence* New York: Fontana

McCall, G. and Shields, N. (1986) 'Social & Structural Factors in Family Violence' in Mary Lystad ed. *Violence in the Home: Interdisciplinary Perspectives* New York: Brunner/Mazel

McIllhatton, S. (1984) 'Domestic Violence: Remedies Under New South Wales and Federal Legislation' *Law Society Journal* August 439–41

McIntyre, D. 'Domestic Violence: A Case of the Disappearing Victim? *Australian Journal of Family Therapy* 1984 5 (4), pp. 249–58

Moore, D. M. ed. *Battered Women* Beverly Hills: Sage

National Committee on Violence (1990) *Violence: Directions for Australia* Australian Institute of Criminology

Newton, A. 'Violent Marriage' *Australian Journal of Family Therapy* 3 (1) 1981, pp. 27–32

Nicarthy, G., Merriam, K. and Coffman, S. (1984) *Talking It Out. A Guide to Groups for Abused Women* Washington: Seal

Noesjirwan, J. (1985) *Evaluation of New South Wales Women's Refuges. Ten Years On* Sydney: New South Wales Women' Refuges Evaluation Steering Committee

New South Wales Domestic Violence Committee (1985) *Report to the Premier of New South Wales* Sydney: New South Wales Women's Co-ordination Unit

New South Wales Government Violence Against Women and Children Law Reform Task Force (1987) *Consultation Paper* Sydney: New South Wales Women's Co-ordination Unit

Office of the Status of Women (1988) *Community Attitudes Towards Domestic Violence in Australia* Sydney. Public Policy Research Centre

Otter, L. 'Domestic Violence: A Feminist Perspective: Implications for Practice' in C. H. Marchant and B. Wearing eds *Gender Reclaimed. Women in Social Work* Marrickville: Hale & Iremonger

Pagelow, M. (1984) *Family Violence* New York: Praeger

Pagelow, M. (1981) *Woman-Battering. Victims and Their Experiences* Beverly Hills: Sage Publications

Pahl, J. ed. (1985) *Private Violence & Public Policy. The Needs of Battered Women & the Response of the Public Services* London: Routledge & Kegan Paul

Prescott, J. (1975) 'Body Pleasure and the Origins of Violence' *The Futurist* April 1975, pp. 64–74

Rada, R. (1978) *Clinical Aspects of the Rapist* New York Grune & Slaton

Renvoize, J. (1978) *Web of Violence. A Study of Family Violence* Harmondsworth: Penguin

Rosenbaum, A. and O'Leary, K. D. (1981) 'Marital Violence: Characteristics of Abusive Couples' *Journal of Consulting & Clinical Psychology* Vol. 49 no. 1, pp. 63–71

Rosenberg, M., Stark, E. and Zahn, M. (1986) 'Interpersonal Violence: Homicide and Spouse Abuse' in J. Last ed. *Public Health & Preventative Medicine* Norwalk: Appleton-Century-Crofts

Rosenblum, K. (1986) 'The Conflict Between & Within Genders: An Appraisal of Contemporary American Femininity & Masculinity' *Sociological Inquiry* Vol. 56 no. 1, pp. 93–104

Rounsaville, B. (1978) 'Theories in Marital Violence: Evidence from a Study of Battered Women' *Victimology* Vol. 3 nos. 1–2, pp. 11–31

Roy, M. ed. (1977) *Battered Women. A Psychosociological Study of Domestic Violence* New York: Van Nostrand Reinhold

Ryan, G., Lane, S., Davis, J. and Isaac, C. (1987) 'Juvenile Sex Offenders: Development and Correction' *Child Abuse & Neglect* Vol. 11 no. 3, pp. 385–95

Schechter, S. (1982) *Women and Violence* Boston: South End Press

Scott, R. and Tetreault, L. (1987) 'Attitudes of Rapists and Other Violent Offenders Toward Women' *The Journal of Social Psychology* 127 (4), pp. 375–80

Scutt J. (1982) 'Domestic Violence: The Police Response' in C. O'Donnell and J. Craney ed. *Family Violence in Australia* Melbourne: Longman Cheshire

Scutt, J. (1983) *Even in the Best of Homes. Violence in the Family* Ringwood: Penguin

Scutt, J. ed. (1980) *Violence in the Family* Canberra: Australian Institute of Crimonology

Shainess, N. (1984) *Sweet Suffering. Woman as Victim* New York: Bobbs-Merrill

Sherman, L. and R. Berk (1984) 'The Specific Deterrent Effects of Arrest for Domestic Assault' *American Sociological Review* Vol. 49, pp. 261–72

Shipley, S. and Sylvester, D. 'Professionals' Attitudes Towards Violence in Close Relationships' *Journal of Emergency Nursing* March–April 1982, 8 (2), pp. 88–91

Smith, A. 'Women's Refuges: the Only Resort?' in Don Barry and Peter Botsman eds *Public/Private* Sydney: Local Consumption Publications

Sonkin, D. ed. (1987) *Domestic Violence on Trial* New York: Springer

Sonkin, D. and Durphy, M. (1985) *Learning to Live Without Violence. A Handbook for Men* San Francisco: Volcano Press

Sonkin, D., Martin, D. and Walker, L. (1985) *The Male Batterer. A Treatment Approach* New York: Springer

Stanko, E. (1985) *Intimate Intrusions. Women's Experience of Male Violence* London: Routledge & Kegan Paul

Stannard, B. 'Domestic Violence. The Problem We Don't Talk About' *The Bulletin* 11 August 1987, pp. 56–61

Star, B. (1983) *Helping the Abuser. Intervening Effectively in Family Violence* New York: Family Service Association of America

Stark, E. and Flitcraft, A. 'Personal Power & Institutional Victimization: Treating the Dual Trauma of Woman Battering' in F. Ochberg ed. (1988) *Post-Traumatic Therapy & Victims of Violence* New York: Brunner/ Mazel

Stark, E., Flitcraft, A. and Frazier, W. 'Medicine & Patriarchal Violence: The Social Construction of a "Private" Event' *International Journal of Health Services* 1979, Vol. 9 (3), pp. 461–93

Stark, R. and McEvoy, J. (1970) 'Middle Class Violence' *Psychology Today* 4, pp. 52–65

Steley, J. (1990) 'Sexually Abusive Callers in the Context of Crisis Agencies: A Literature Review' *Australian Journal of Marriage & Family* Vol. 11 (1), pp. 19–27

Storr, A. (1978) Introduction to J. Eekelaar and S. Katz eds *Family Violence. An International & Interdisciplinary Study* Toronto: Butterworths

Straus, M. (1977) 'A Sociological Perspective on the Prevention & Treatment of Wifebeating' in M. Roy, ed. *Battered Women* New York: Van Nostrand

Straus, M. (1978) 'Wife-beating: How Common and Why' in J. Eekelaar and N. Katz eds *Family Violence. An International and Interdisciplinary Study* Toronto: Butterworths

Straus, M. and Gelles, R. 'Societal Change & Change in Family Violence from 1975 to 1985 As Revealed by Two National Surveys' *Journal of Marriage & the Family* August 1986 (48), pp. 465–79

Straus, M., Gelles, R. and Steinmetz, S. (1980) *Behind Closed Doors* New York: Anchor Books

Stubbs, J. and Wallace, A. (1988) 'Protecting Victims of Domestic Violence?' in M. Findlay and R. Hogg eds *Understanding Crime & Criminal Justice* Sydney: The Law Book Company

Swift, C. (1986) 'Preventing Family Violence: Family-Focused Programs' in M. Lystad, ed. *Violence in the Home: Interdisciplinary Perspectives* New York: Brunner/Mazel

Taubman, S. 'Beyond the Bravado: Sex Roles & the Exploitive Male' *Social Work* January-February 1986, Vol. 31 (1), pp. 12–18

Tierney, K. 'The Battered Women Movement and the Creation of the Wife Beating Problem' *Social Problems* February 1982, Vol. 29 (3), pp. 209–20

Toby, J. (1974) 'Violence and the Masculine Ideal' in S. Steinmetz and M. Straus eds *Violence in the Family* New York: Harper & Row

Van Hasselt, V., Morrison, R. and Bellack, A. (1985) 'Alcohol Use in Wife Abusers and their Spouses' *Addictive Behaviors* Vol. 10, pp. 127–35
Walker, L. (1979) *The Battered Woman* New York: Harper & Row
Walker, L. (1984) *The Battered Woman Syndrome* New York: Springer
Walker, L. and Browne, A. (1985) 'Gender and Victimization by Intimates' *Journal of Personality* Vol. 53 no. 2, pp. 179–95
Walker, L. (1986) 'Psychological Causes of Family Violence' in M. Lystad ed. *Violence in the Home* New York: Brunner/Mazel
Walker-Hooper, A. (1981) 'Domestic Violence: Assessing the Problem' in C. Warner ed. *Conflict Intervention in Social and Domestic Violence* London: Prentice-Hall
Wehner, D. (1986) 'Working With Violent Men. Issues, Programs and Training' in S. Hatty ed. *Proceedings, National Conference on Domestic Violence* November 1985, Canberra: Australian Institute of Criminology
Weitzman, J. and Dreen, K. 'Wife Beating: A View of the Marital Dyad' *Social Casework* May 1982, pp. 259–65
Whitehurst, R. (1974) 'Violence in Husband-Wife Interaction' in S. Steinmetz and M. Straus eds *Violence in the Family* New York: Harper & Row

PATRIARCHY/POWER
Bachrach, P. and Baratz, M. (1979) *Power & Poverty. Theory & Practice* New York: Oxford University Press
Barrett, M. and McIntosh, M. (1985) *The Anti-Social Family* London: Verso
Burton, C. (1985) *Subordination. Feminism & Social Theory* Sydney: George Allen & Unwin
Cass, B. (1983) 'Population Policies & Family Policies: State Construction of Domestic Life' in C. Baldock and B. Cass eds *Women, Social Welfare & the State* Sydney: George Allen & Unwin
Conley, J. (1988) 'Violence on TV May Be Curbed' *The Age* 9 June 1988, p. 1
Delphy, C. and Leonard, D. (1986) 'Class Analysis, Gender Analysis and the Family' in R. Crompton and M. Mann eds *Gender and Stratification* Oxford: Basil Blackwell
Edwards, M. (1980) 'Social Effects of Taxation' in J. Wilkes ed. *The Politics of Taxation* Lane Cove: Hodder & Staoghton
Eisenstein, Z. ed. (1979) *Capitalism, Patriarchy & the Case for Socialist Feminism* New York: Monthly Review Press
Game, A. and Pringle, R. (1983) *Gender At Work* Sydney: George Allen & Unwin
Hamilton, R. (1978) *The Liberation of Women. A Study of Patriarchy & Capitalism* London: George Allen & Unwin
Keens, C. and Cass, B. (1982) *Fiscal Welfare: Some Aspects of Australian Tax Policy. Class and Gender Considerations* Sydney: Social Welfare Research Centre
Kewley, T. (1980) *Australian Social Security Today. Major Developments from 1900 to 1978* Sydney: Sydney University Press
Knuckey, D. (1990) 'Equality at Work Remains Elusive' The *Australian* 3 February 1990, p. 46
Mackinnon, C. (1987) *Feminism Unmodified. Discourses on Life & Law* Massachusetts: Harvard University Press

Pateman, C. (1988) *The Sexual Contract* Cambridge: Polity Press

Phelps, L. (1981) 'Patriarchy and Capitalism' in Essays from Quest *Building Feminist Theory* New York: Longman

Roe, J. (1983) 'The End is Where We Start From: Women and Welfare Since 1901' in C. Baldock and B. Cass *Women, Social Welfare & the State* Sydney: George Allen & Unwin

Shaver, S. (1983) 'Sex and Money in the Welfare State' in C. Baldock and B. Cass eds *Women, Social Welfare & the State* Sydney: George Allen & Unwin

Stacey, M. and Price, M. (1981) *Women, Power & Politics* London: Tavistock

Zaretsky, E. (1976) *Capitalism, The Family & Personal Life* New York: Harper Colophon

THE MODERN FAMILY

Amato, P. (1987) *Children in Australian Families: The Growth of Competence* Sydney: Prentice-Hall

Bell, C. and Newby, H. (1976) 'Husbands and Wives: The Dynamics of the Deferential Dialectic' in D. Barker and S. Allen eds *Dependence & Exploitation in Work & Marriage* London: Longman

Bittman, M. 'What's Modern About the Modern Family?' Paper presented to The Australian Sociological Association Conference, La Trobe University, 8–12 December 1989

Blumstein, P. and Schwartz, P. (1983) *American Couples, Money, Work, Sex* New York: William Morrow

Buri, J., Kirchner, P. and Walsh, J. (1987) 'Familial Correlates of Self-Esteem in Young American Adults' *The Journal of Social Psychology* 127 (6), pp. 583–8

English, B. A. and King R. J. (1983) *Families in Australia* Sydney: Bridge Printery

Epstein, S. (1980) 'The Self-concept' in E. Staub ed. *Personality: Basic Issues and Current Research* New York: Prentice-Hall

Fromm, E. (1982) *The Art of Loving* London: Allen & Unwin

Gittins, D. (1986) *The Family in Question. Changing Households & Familiar Ideologies* Basingstoke: Macmillan

Hafner, R. J. (1986) *Marriage and Mental Illness. A Sex-Roles Perspective* New York: Guilford Press

Hall, B., Lamont, L., Mackintosh, J. and St John, W. (1987) 'A Guide Book for Teaching Parenting *The Australian Nurses Journal* Vol. 17 no. 4, pp. 52–5

Jacobsen, E. (1980) *The Self and the Object World* 5th edn New York: International Universities Press

Land, H. (1978) 'Who Cares for the Family?' *Journal of Social Policy* 7, no. 3, pp. 257–84

Morgan, D. H. J. (1985) *The Family, Politics & Social Theory* London: Routledge & Kegan Paul

Pelham, B. and Swann, W. (1989) 'From Self-Conceptions to Self-Worth: On the Sources & Structures of Global Self-Esteem' *Journal of Personality & Social Psychology* Vol. 57 no. 4, pp. 672–80

Poster, M. (1982) *Critical Theory of the Family* London: Pluto Press

Rubin, L. (1983) *Intimate Strangers. Men and Women Together* New York: Harper & Row

Scanzoni, L. and Scanzoni, J. (1976) *Men, Women and Change. A Sociology of Marriage and Family* New York: McGraw-Hill

GENDER

Abbott, F. ed. (1987) *New Men, New Minds* Freedom: The Crossing Press

Allen, J. (1988) 'The Masculinity of Criminality and Criminology: Interrogating Some Impasses' in M. Findlay and R. Hogg eds *Understanding Crime & Criminal Justice* Sydney: The Law Book Company

Brod, H. ed. (1987) *The Making of Masculinities* Boston: Allen & Unwin

Chesler, P. (1978) *About Men* London: The Women's Press

Chodorow, N. (1978) *The Reproduction of Mothering. Psychoanalysis and the Sociology of Gender* Berkeley: University of California Press

Connell, R. (1987) *Gender & Power* Sydney: Allen & Unwin

Conway, R. (1984) *The End of the Stupour?* Melbourne: Macmillan

Craib, I. (1987) 'Masculinity and Male Dominance' *Social Problems* 34 (5), pp. 721–43

Dinnerstein, D. (1978) *The Rocking of the Cradle, and the Ruling of the World* London: Souvenir Press (Educational & Academic)

Donaldson, M. (1987) 'Labouring Men: Love, Sex and Strife' *Australian & New Zealand Journal of Sociology* Vol. 23 no. 2, pp. 165–84

Fasteau, M. (1975) *The Male Machine* N.Y., Delta

Feldman, L. (1985) 'Sex Roles and Family Dynamics' in F. Walsh ed. *Normal Family Processes* New York: Guilford Press

Filene, P. (1987) 'The Secrets of Men's History' in H. Brod ed. *The Making of Masculinities* Boston: Allen & Unwin

Fletcher, R. (1988) 'Non-Sexist Education for Boys' *Education* 30 June 1988, p. 24

Hearn, J. (1985) 'Men's Sexuality at Work' in A. Metcalfe and M. Humphries eds *The Sexuality of Men* London: Pluto Press

Hunt, J. and Rudden, M. (1986) 'Gender Differences in the Psychology of Parenting: Psychoanalytic and Feminist Perspectives' *Journal of The American Academy of Psychoanalysis* 14 (2), pp. 213–25

Krull, M. (1987) *Freud & His Father* London: W.W. Norton & Company

Lemle, R. and Mishkind, M. (1989) 'Alcohol & Masculinity' *Journal of Substance Abuse Treatment* Vol. 6, pp. 213–22

Messner, M. (1987) 'The Meaning of Success: The Athletic Experience & the Development of Male Identity' in H. Brod ed. *The Making of Masculinities* Boston: Allen & Unwin

Metcalf, A. and Humphries, M. eds (1985) *The Sexuality of Men* London: Pluto Press

Miller, S. (1983) *Men & Friendship* Bath: Gateway

Person, E. (1980) 'Sexuality as the Mainstay of Identity: Psychoanalytic Perspectives' in C. Stimpson and E. Person eds *Women, Sex and Sexuality* Chicago: University of Chicago Press

Pleck, J. (1981) *The Myth of Masculinity* Cambridge: Massachusetts Institute of Technology Press

Seidler, V. (1985) 'Fear and Intimacy' in A. Metcalf and M. Humphries eds *The Sexuality of Men* London: Pluto Press

Tolson, A. (1977) *The Limits of Masculinity* London: Tavistock

Ullian, D. (1981) 'Why Boys Will Be Boys' *American Journal of Orthopsychiatry* 51 (3), pp. 493–501

Weedon, C. (1987) *Feminist Practice & Postructuralist Theory* Oxford: Basil Blackwell

Young, I. (1983) 'Is Male Gender Identity the Cause of Male Domination?' in J. Trebilcot ed. *Mothering. Essays in Feminist Theory* Totowa, Rowman & Allanheld

Index

nonassertiveness, 47; professional attitudes to, 26–8; victim blaming, 1; *see also* battery; violence against women
Williams, Claire, 83
Willis, Paul, 81
wives, dysfunctional behaviour, 43; emotional dependence of, 119–20; labour participation, 30; violence against, 22–4; *see also* wife battery
woman, as class, 17; as sex, 17
women, power over, and masculinity, 86–7; status of, in society, 119

work, 19–22; and family conflict, 121; gender segregation, 81; hierarchy, and self-esteem, 83; and male identity, 81, 82; male solidarity, sexual harassment, 82; and masculinity, 80–7 *passim*; preparation for, 109–10; sexual equality at, 97
working class, male chauvinism, 83; masculinity, 72; stereotypical masculine traits, 127; work hierarchy, and self-esteem, 82–3
workplace, as male domain, 121

Zaretsky, Eli, 18, 20, 37